Rhythms of Reformation

"*Rhythms of Reformation* is a clarion call to wakefulness, a wake-up jolt to churches stumbling through the post-COVID wilderness. Like a skilled jazz improviser riffing on a familiar tune, the author takes us on a wild ride of autoethnographic storytelling, exposing the dirty little secret of our Sunday-centric, consumerist Christianity. But here's the twist: this book isn't just a jeremiad; it's a gospel invitation to revival. By laying out four discipleship beats—Temple, Table, Technology, and Training—the author gives us a practical primer for rebooting the church's discipleship machinery. This ain't your grandma's attractional model; this is about igniting self-initiated spirituality that sets believers free to jam with God in the midst of life's messy rhythms. *Rhythms of Reformation* is less a diagnosis of the church's pandemic-induced paralysis and more a prophetic map for charting a new course—one that burns the bridges of yesterday's irrelevance and finds its footing in the untamed rhythms of reformation. For church leaders willing to take the leap, this book offers a Spirit-led road map for reimagining the church in this uncharted era."

—LEONARD SWEET, author of *Decoding the Divine*

"Garth Ball is a man with a godly passion to see discipleship restored to its rightful, preeminent place in the church worldwide. When Jesus said, 'Go and make disciples' (Matt 28:18–20), he didn't mean 'go and attract crowds' or 'go and build an empire.' He genuinely intended for his disciples to reproduce his life in others, forming true image-bearers of Jesus himself. As Garth's thesis supervisor, I witnessed firsthand his deep understanding of the church and his compelling response to the post-COVID need for a return to authentic disciple-making. This shift—from focusing on attractional models to embracing transformational discipleship—is powerfully articulated in his book, *Rhythms of Reformation*. This is a must-read for every pastor, leader, and Christian. Those who engage with it will be impacted, empowered, and transformed to live as true disciple-makers."

—DARYL J. POTTS, Lecturer, School of Ministry and Theology, Alphacrucis University College, Australia

"*Rhythms of Reformation* is a timely and prophetic call to the church to move beyond consumerism and Sunday-centric models into the vibrant, Spirit-led rhythms of true discipleship. Garth Ball lays a practical and Spirit-breathed foundation for leaders who desire to cultivate Kingdom culture, not just host events. His framework—Temple, Table, Technology, and Training—offers a compelling vision for building ecosystems that multiply disciples and reestablish Christ at the center. This book is a critical resource for pastors, pioneers, and reformers who know the Church must not go back to business-as-usual. Read it, wrestle with it, and reform with it."

—GLENN BLEAKNEY, Founder, Awake Nations, Sunshine Coast, Australia

"In this timely and thoughtful work, Garth Ball brings a pastoral and prophetic burden to bear on one of the most urgent questions facing the twenty-first-century church: What is God saying to us in the aftermath of the global disruption of COVID-19? Drawing from reflective practice, experiential learning, and dialogue among trusted practitioners, he presents a courageous call to reformation. Reformation is a weighty and provocative word—one that speaks of necessary change, purification, and realignment so the church might once again reflect its God-given purpose. Throughout church history, faithful leaders have recognized the apostolic task of returning to biblical patterns of leadership and mission, seeking alignment with the original mandate of Scripture. With an apostolic mindset and prophetic edge, Garth explores the sociological, psychological, and spiritual terrain of our moment, offering fresh insight into the transition the church is undergoing. This work is a valuable resource for leaders and practitioners who long to navigate this season with clarity, conviction, and courage. I commend it wholeheartedly."

—PHIL AND JULIE OLDFIELD, Senior Ministers, C3 Church Tuggerah

"In this timely and thoughtful book, Garth offers a reflective vision of post-COVID church leadership—marked not by critique alone, but by invitation and hope. He models a team-based, vulnerable approach that resists the superhero leader stereotype. His embrace of reformation as a rhythm, a kind of *semper reformanda*, invites churches into ongoing Spirit-shaped renewal. Rather than returning to what was, Garth calls us to faithfully adapt to what is. At its heart is a deep conviction: that discipleship is the God-given mission for every church in every age. This is a wise, pastoral work for leaders navigating the shifting realities of our time."

—RYAN KERRISON, Lecturer, School of Ministry and Theology, Alphacrucis University College, Australia

"In *Rhythms of Reformation*, Garth offers a compelling and deeply practical framework for navigating the challenges faced by the church today, especially in our post-pandemic world. He masterfully utilizes Richard R. Osmer's four tasks of practical theology, an approach that allows for an engaging exploration of the current discipleship landscape and the urgent need for a new reformation and culture within the church. This book is more than just theological reflection; it's a guide to cultivating a 'self-initiated spirituality' and building 'future-proof' churches that will endure for generations. Garth respectfully examines past church models and practices while prophetically calling for a stronger, more intentional return to biblical discipleship—an essential shift for any leader serious about fulfilling the Great Commission. I highly recommend *Rhythms of Reformation* to every leader and church worker. Don't just read it; wrestle with its truths, process it with your team, and apply its wisdom to see genuine, transformative growth in your church and ministry."

—BRETT BARCLAY, Hope Unlimited Church, Australia

Rhythms of Reformation

Returning the Church to the Heartbeat of Discipleship

GARTH BALL

Foreword by Julius Rwotlonyo

WIPF & STOCK · Eugene, Oregon

RHYTHMS OF REFORMATION
Returning the Church to the Heartbeat of Discipleship

Wipf & Stock
An Imprint of Wipf and Stock Publishers
199 W. 8th Ave., Suite 3
Eugene, OR 97401

www.wipfandstock.com

PAPERBACK ISBN: 979-8-3852-3141-6
HARDCOVER ISBN: 979-8-3852-3142-3
EBOOK ISBN: 979-8-3852-3143-0

07/08/25

Contents

CONTENTS

Foreword

I HAVE HAD THE joy and responsibility of serving in pastoral ministry for almost two decades, all of them within the church I now have the honor of leading alongside my wife, Vernita. Since 2016, I have served in a senior leadership capacity, and through-out these years, I have witnessed many seasons in the life of the church—some fruitful, others stretching—but nothing could have prepared me for the seismic shift that came with COVID-19. In our context, we often speak of life in three eras: *Before COVID* (BC), *During COVID* (DC), and *After COVID* (AC). Each of these periods brought its own challenges, but DC and AC were by far the most disruptive. Globally, pastors left the ministry in large num-bers, congregations dwindled, and some churches, sadly, closed their doors for good. It was a sobering time that tested our very understanding of what it means to be the church.

And yet, amid the shaking, there were those who endured. Some longed for the return of the "good old days," hoping to rees-tablish what was familiar. Others slipped into a survival mentality, holding on with quiet desperation, hoping things would eventually improve. But then there was another group—leaders and churches who recognized that God was doing something new and who were willing to learn from the disruption, pivot in obedience, and press forward with renewed conviction and clarity. Garth's book, *Rhythms of Reformation*, is relevant for all three groups, offering language, frameworks, and wisdom to lead faithfully in this post-pandemic world.

I have had the privilege of knowing Garth and his wife, Jaime, for many years. I first met Garth before he planted his first church in Nairobi, and since then, I have watched him expand that work across three diverse cities—Nairobi, Newcastle, and Dubai. His ability to raise leaders and cultivate health in congregations across such varied cultural and spiritual landscapes exemplifies Garth's apostolic leadership calling.

During the COVID-19 season, I was personally strengthened by Garth's prophetic insights, as we both navigated those unprecedented times. I am thrilled that he has now documented those insights in this new book. One conversation, in particular, stayed with me. I vividly recall Garth speaking of four key environments that shape a disciple-making church: (1) Temple, (2) Table, (3) Technology, and (4) Training. This both affirmed what we were already doing as a church while also challenging us to execute these areas with equal strength. At Watoto Church, we were strong in the Temple and Table environments—but we knew we had to grow in our use of Technology and reimagine our Training models. We began to shift from event-based approaches to more outcome-based discipleship strategies.

This book provides a simple yet profound framework of thought for church leaders who desire genuine growth—growth that is both quantitative and qualitative and that can withstand the storms and challenges that may come. Garth builds on the work of Richard R. Osmer's *Practical Theology: An Introduction*, using Osmer's four tasks to frame his exploration: (1) descriptive-empirical: "What is going on?"; (2) interpretive: "Why is this going on?"; (3) normative: "What ought to be going on?"; and (4) pragmatic: "How might we respond?" Garth's work delves deeply into these questions, and its findings may surprise some readers, spark many aha moments, challenge conventional paradigms, and, most importantly, provide practical guidance for anyone committed to fulfilling our Master's Great Commission: "Go and make disciples of all nations" (Matt 28:18–20).

To every pastor, church leader, planter, and visionary who is serious about building a legacy, I urge you to read this book. By "legacy," I mean making disciples who will make disciples of others, and building "future-proof" churches that will endure for generations. Do not just read it—wrestle with it, pray through it, and process it with your team. Then apply what is relevant to your context. And finally, pass it on. Buy a copy for a younger leader you are mentoring, or a peer you are walking with. Because the truth is, we are not competitors—we are collaborators. We are one church, with one Captain—Jesus—and one goal: to see the whole earth filled with the knowledge of the glory of God, as the waters cover the sea (Hab 2:14).

JULIUS RWOTLONYO
Team Leader | Watotc Church

Introduction

AN UNPRECEDENTED DECADE

It is difficult to find words that adequately describe the COVID-19 pandemic's profound impact on humanity. Despite its overuse causing some linguistic fatigue, "unprecedented" has been the word of choice to attempt this task, uniquely encapsulating this once-in-a-generation phenomenon.[1] So widespread was the word's resonance that it was named People's Choice 2020 Word of the Year at Dictionary.com and was included in the title of Oxford Language's annual report, *2020: Words of an Unprecedented Year*.[2] The word was apt in that the spread of the virus—along with containment measures such as social isolations—impacted public health, education, economic, religious, and other sectors in ways not seen since World War II.[3]

The British Academy provides an unsettling forecast regarding societal recovery from the COVID-19 pandemic, writing, "We are in a COVID decade: the social, economic and cultural effects of the pandemic will cast a long shadow into the future–perhaps longer than a decade–and the sooner we begin to understand, the

1. Valdes, "Reflection and Change," 160.
2. Eubanks, "Unprecedented"; Oxford Languages, *Unprecedented Year*.
3. Yan, "Unprecedented Pandemic," 110.

better placed we will be to address them."[4] The global church is not exempt from such a pathway to recovery. Karl Vaters predicts that while the church entered the pandemic suddenly, it would come out only through a "long, slow process of retraining."[5] This indicates that although we are out of lockdown, we are not out of the woods. It seems likely that what lies ahead will be an unprecedented decade.

EMERGING POST-COVID CONVERSATIONS

Since the onset of the COVID-19 pandemic and the initial wave of lockdowns, a growing body of literature has explored the church's response and adaptation to this global crisis. One theme to emerge, for example, has centered around justice, with the pandemic "significantly worsening an already serious global gap in access to justice."[6] Gender-based violence increased significantly during COVID-19 in numerous countries—such as China, South Africa, and the United States—with more women and girls being confined to their homes through lockdown.[7] The poor have been disproportionately affected by the pandemic, with ninety-seven million more people living in extreme poverty than before 2020.[8] Systemic injustices and corruption were illuminated in African countries such as South Africa, Kenya, and Nigeria, with COVID-19 aid money plundered by the already rich and powerful.[9] In the United States, Black and Indigenous communities as well as other communities of people of color were affected disproportionately due to several economic, social, and vocational

---

4. British Academy, "COVID Decade," 6.
5. Vaters, "Pastoring After COVID."
6. World Justice Project, *COVID-19 Pandemic*, 3.
7. John et al., "Lessons Never Learned," 66.
8. World Relief, "COVID-19 Impact," 5.
9. Kaunda, "Need to Rethink," 326.

factors.[10] Amid these sobering realizations, Christian voices are calling the church to meaningful action in the post-COVID era.[11]

Mental health is another dominant theme within post-COVID literature. Although several authors identify mental health as a difficult area to assess over a short period of time, there is enough evidence to discern worrying trends of increased mental illness.[12] Dalmacito A. Cordero Jr. observed increased levels of anxiety and depression in college students in the Philippines during the pandemic. Liang, Sun, and Tang report "severe symptoms of anxiety, depression, post-traumatic stress disorder, psychological distress, and stress . . . in the general population during the COVID-19 pandemic in China, Spain, Italy, Iran, the USA, Turkey, Nepal, and Denmark."[13] Several reports of declined mental health during the pandemic came from Australia, noting causes from both the virus itself and the lockdowns that resulted.[14] The ministerial pressures of leading through the COVID-19 crisis have ensured that church leaders have not been immune, with Barna Group reporting in March 2022 that 42 percent of pastors in the United States had seriously considered leaving their job over the preceding twelve-month period—a significant rise from the 29 percent reported in January 2021.[15]

Just as it is difficult to definitively identify the effect of COVID-19 on mental health to date, so too is it challenging to predict its ongoing impact.[16] The primary idea in existing literature around the future of mental health, however, is that the negative effects of COVID-19 have not disappeared with the end of COVID-19 as a global public health emergency. John Eldredge warns, "We haven't yet paid the psychological bill for all we've been

10. Li, "Racial Disparities."

11. For example Pillay, "Church More Flexible," 270.

12. Liang et al., "Mental Health Research," 1.

13. Liang et al., "Mental Health Research," 7.

14. Headspace, "Coping with COVID," 2; Zhao et al., "COVID-19," 2.

15. Barna Group, "Pastors Share."

16. Liang et al., "Mental Health Research," 11.

through."[17] Leonard Sweet agrees, calling our experience a "collective trauma."[18] This has significant implications for the church, with much work needing to be done to help both church leaders and church members walk into more positive levels of health.

PRACTICAL THEOLOGY AND ANALYTIC AUTOETHNOGRAPHY

Important conversations around digital and missional expressions of church are also shaping post-COVID ecclesiology. They will be referenced throughout this book insofar as they have helped shape its major idea: a call to return discipleship to the center of church theory and practice. Amid the chorus of voices seeking to interpret and respond to the COVID-19 pandemic, God was drawing me into a journey of understanding that was uniquely my own—one centered on discipleship and one that would shatter many of my long-held convictions about congregational ministry. This book tells that story, which entails my experience of leading Rhythm City Church—at that time a church with locations in Nairobi, Kenya, and Newcastle, Australia—through the COVID-19 pandemic. While this work is rooted in personal experience, it is not merely a memoir. Rather, it takes the form of an analytic autoethnography, with personal narrative serving as a vehicle for theological interpretation.

Adams, Ellis, and Jones define autoethnography as "a research method that uses personal experience ('auto') to describe and interpret ('graphy') cultural texts, experiences, beliefs, and practices ('ethno')."[19] L. DiAnne Borders and Amanda L. Giordano describe the difference between two types of autoethnography, writing, "Analytic autoethnography differs from evocative autoethnography in that it analyzes and generalizes the data rather than providing

17. Eldredge, *Resilient*, xi.
18. Sweet, "Semiotic Exegesis," 3.
19. Adams et al., "Autoethnography," 1.

personal reflections only."[20] The following narrative adopts an analytic approach, weaving my personal experience together with critical engagement across a wide body of precedent literature.

The narrative is personal in nature and was selected from among other possible approaches, such as a *co-constructed narrative* that focuses on the relational interactions within a story.[21] I seriously considered a co-constructed narrative, as a significant part of my leadership response to the COVID-19 pandemic involved a collaboration with the leadership teams in our churches. As I developed post-COVID ecclesiological insights, I brought them to the teams who formed a working group to both critique the validity of the ideas and brainstorm the outworking of them in the church community. While I am indebted to the teams who co-labored with me in this work, much of the innovation emerged from my own leadership reflection. As such, this autoethnography centers on my experience of carrying the weight of senior leadership at Rhythm City Church through the challenges of the COVID-19 pandemic.

The narrative in this analytic autoethnography is organized according to Richard R. Osmer's four tasks of practical theology. Although not all agree, a significant number of practical theologians suggest that theological reflection in this field frequently begins with human experience rather than belief.[22] This initiates a cyclical process, in which theological reflection not only informs practice but is also, at times, reshaped by it. Osmer interprets the four tasks of practical theology as: (1) the *descriptive-empirical task*, answering the question "What is going on?"; (2) the *interpretive task*, asking the question "Why is this going on?"; (3) the *normative task*, inquiring, "What ought to be going on?"; and (4) the *pragmatic task*, finally exploring "How might we respond?"[23] Although not cognizant of it at the time, these tasks closely mirror the journey I undertook in response to the initial stages of the

20. Borders and Giordano, "Confronting Confrontation," 455.

21. Ellis, *Ethnographic I*, 71.

22. Swinton and Mowatt, *Practical Theology*, 6.

23. Osmer, *Practical Theology*, 4.

COVID-19 pandemic. The analysis of precedent literature within this narrative represents a continuation of that practical theological inquiry.

There are several key contributions I hope this book will make to the lives of its readers. Firstly, although the official global health emergency has ended, the effects of the pandemic continue to reverberate throughout both individual and societal life, leaving significant work still to be done for recovery.[24] One meaningful contribution to this ongoing process is the act of giving voice to the diverse lived experiences of the COVID-19 pandemic through autoethnography. As Ellis, Adams, and Bochner propose, personal narratives can carry therapeutic value—not only for the storyteller but also for those who listen—offering a space for healing, reflection, and shared understanding.[25]

Secondly, the shared narrative offers an invitation: "To enter the author's world and to use what they learn there to reflect on, understand, and cope with their own lives."[26] For many church leaders navigating the practical implications of post-COVID ecclesiology, an insider's perspective provides more than outcomes—it reveals the process of adapting to change in a new era. This may be especially helpful for current and emerging leaders who have discerned the reformational opportunity COVID-19 presented but remain uncertain about how to lead their communities into that new reality.

Although this story started with the COVID-19 pandemic, it is by no means limited to it. COVID-19 will not be the last kairos moment available to the church. Reformation must become a rhythm—an ongoing pattern of aligning our life and ministry with the heart of God. For those reading this long after the COVID-19 decade has passed, the reflections within these pages are intended to serve as a timeless road map for cultivating a reformational culture and navigating the many winds of change that will continue to shape the church in the future.

24. Mooallem, "Three Years into Covid."
25. Ellis et al., "Autoethnography," 280.
26. Ellis et al., "Autoethnography," 280.

COVID-19 ERA VS. POST-COVID ERA

A final word regarding terminology. In this work, the COVID-19
era is defined as spanning from January 30, 2020, when the World
Health Organization (WHO) declared the COVID-19 outbreak a
public health emergency of international concern, to May 5, 2023,
when the WHO lifted the global health emergency designation.[27]
The post-COVID era is defined as the period commencing May 5,
2023, and onward. When referencing the post-COVID ecclesiological era, I am concerned with the implementation of ministry
changes informed by insights that emerged during the pandemic.
This focus moves beyond the immediate ecclesiological responses
of the COVID-19 era, which primarily involved pivoting to digital
expressions of church life due to social isolation measures.

Although a distinction is made between the COVID-19 and
post-COVID eras, my journey of reflection necessarily weaves between them. Much of the work carried out under the descriptive-
empirical, interpretive, and normative tasks of practical theology
took place during the COVID-19 era. Similarly, while many of the
ideas explored in the pragmatic task emerged within that same
time frame, their implementation is oriented toward the ongoing
realities of the post-COVID era.

27. Wise, "Covid-19," 1.

1

God Speaks from the Whirlwind

"When the lockdown ends, we cannot go back to how things were. I am not sure what we were doing was working too well anyway."

THESE WORDS FROM A respected church leader about the church's possible response to the COVID-19 pandemic deeply impacted me. I had heard similar suggestions in the whirlwind of those initial weeks of March 2020 but had not given the idea serious consideration.[1] Like most church leaders, the administrative hustle of pivoting to online weekend services was taking every ounce of energy and attention.[2] The cumulative effect of this emerging narrative became evident, however, as this statement provoked resistance within me.

"That is all good and well to say, but what do you propose that looks like?" I mumbled under my breath watching the Instagram live. "Some of us have churches to run and need some

---

1. See Costea, *19 Covid Lessons,* 17–19.
2. For example, see Johnston et al., "Pastoral Ministry," 376.

practical solutions, not idealistic philosophies sprouted from an ivory tower." A rational—maybe even divine—inner voice arose louder within me than the noise of my grumbling, and I knew I had an important decision to make. Would I ignore this provocation from someone I respected for their prophetic clarity regarding ecclesiological issues, or would I do the hard work of leaning into the heart of God for this cultural moment?

Without hesitation, I made an internal commitment to the latter, not foreseeing the significance of either the journey ahead or the conclusions it would produce. The process of practical theology that followed dislodged me from the treadmill of ecclesiological theories and practices I had inherited, dramatically and permanently changing the focus of my congregational ministry assignment. The framework of practical theology used in this process originated from Richard R. Osmer, who identifies four tasks of practical theology: (1) the descriptive-empirical task, (2) the interpretive task, (3) the normative task, and (4) the pragmatic task.[3]

3. Osmer, *Practical Theology*, 4.

2

The Descriptive-Empirical Task (1)

A Discipleship Crisis

OSMER NOTES THAT THE *descriptive-empirical task* involves gathering information to answer the question "What is going on?"[1] After the catalytic experience mentioned above, this task aptly describes my initial response in seeking God's heart for the church at this moment. I wanted to understand not only what was evident and observable within the church but, more importantly, what that signified for God's divine purposes. Two realities soon became apparent, one sobering and the other stimulating.

At a combined church event after the first round of lockdowns in Australia, I was unpacking some of my initial observations with the senior leader of a global church movement. He listened patiently as I summarized my views and then gave a response that was short, yet profound. "It is all about one word really, *discipleship.*" This word was not new or unfamiliar, but it struck a chord deep in my soul, and it immediately became clear to me that the response of many Christians during COVID-19-related lockdowns was revealing a discipleship crisis within the church. What made this realization sobering was that this crisis was not

---

1. Osmer, *Practical Theology* 4.

3

just happening within *the* church or *someone else's* church but *my* church. Although "making disciples" appeared on paper in our church mission statement, there appeared to be a significant gap between the value we wrote down and the response being modeled by many of our congregation members.

One of the major indications of this crisis was the consistent decline in online service attendance throughout the lockdown period. When the pivot to online services was first introduced, there was energy among the congregation and people gathered in high numbers. Thom Rainer noticed a similarly positive response in the United States, with many churches galvanizing in the early stages of the crisis.[2] Whether the motivation for this initial attendance was novelty, curiosity, or a genuine value of church gatherings, it did not take long for this trend to reverse for many of our church members. No matter what efforts were employed by church leadership—such as offering to pay for data to counter accessibility issues—many resisted the call to gather, and attendance gradually and consistently decreased throughout the lockdown period.[3] The Barna Group reported that 32 percent of previously practicing Christians also stopped attending services within three months of lockdowns in the United States, showing it was not an isolated experience for Rhythm City Church.[4]

This was a frustrating and painful season in my pastoral ministry journey. Not only was the team at Rhythm City Church spending significant time and energy on creating services that numerous people were not utilizing, but I had anticipated the church to rally together in the face of crisis to be a community of strength and solidarity. Instead, I often heard statements like, "I do not really enjoy church online" as reasons for nonengagement. It was not surprising to me that people would prefer a physical church environment over a digital one; the Barna Group reports that 81

---

2. Rainer, *Simple Church*, 16.

3. Accessibility to internet was prohibitive for the poor through the COVID-19 pandemic. See Mpofu, "Mission on the Margins," 3.

4. Barna Group, "One in Three."

percent of churched adults hold that preference.[5] What was per-
plexing to me was seeing people choose *no* church environment
over a digital one, and how personal preference became a stronger
motivation than a passion for the gathered church. This was a confronting realization about the state of discipleship in our church.

This is not to say that the decline in attendance was the
only sign of a discipleship crisis during the lockdown period,
but it was the most obvious, and one that is indicative of other
health measures. For example, Svob, Murphy, Wickramaratne,
Gameroff, Talati, van Dijk, Yangchen, and Weissman report that
"religious attendance online during the pandemic was associated
with decreased depression and anxiety."[6] Research conducted by
the Barna Group made similar findings.[7] Nor does it mean that
church attendance alone is an indication of spiritual maturity. I
would argue, however, that active participation in a local church
is a fundamental characteristic of discipleship. As D. A. Carson
demonstrates, in the New Testament, joining the local church was
inseparable from conversion and baptism.[8]

As I continued to process these observations, it became evident that this discipleship crisis did not arrive with the COVID-19
pandemic but was a preexisting condition in the church. Lefebvre Solange comments on a study by Bozewicz and Boguszewski,
noting that "a person's previous level of religiosity determined
religious engagement during the pandemic."[9] In other words,
what existed before the COVID-19 pandemic was exacerbated
by it. This pattern has also been observed in other socioeconomic
arenas, with negative outcomes for mental health and social in-
equality both predating the COVID-19 pandemic and intensifying
since its onset.[10] In terms of discipleship, this trend is evidenced

5. Barna Group, *Six Questions*, 7.

6. Svob et al., "Pre- and Post-Pandemic," 9.

7. Barna Group, "One in Three."

8. Carson, "Editorial"

9. Lefebvre, "COVID-19 Pandemic," 2.

10. Marshall, "COVID-19 and Religion," 84; Kaunda, "Need to Rethink,"
326.

positively by the response of those who admirably stayed con- nected and present in the local church community throughout the lockdown period. Conversely, the negative effects discussed above indicate that more weight should have been given to the warnings of church leaders like Mike Breen, who have been drawing atten- tion to a discipleship crisis in the Western church since before the COVID-19 pandemic.[11]

11. Breen, *Building a Discipling Culture*, back cover.

3

The Descriptive-Empirical Task (2)

A New Reformation

IN OCTOBER 2017, I delivered a teaching series in Nairobi called "A New Reformation." It was the Protestant Reformation's five hundredth anniversary, and I sensed a fresh reformation was needed in the church. The purpose of the series was to push back on the power imbalances I observed in some churches across the region and to advocate for a renewed emphasis on the priesthood of all believers' theology and praxis.[1] This initial idea about a new reformation in the church seemed to be scattered among church leaders globally. Ken Ham, for example, wrote an article on the eve of the anniversary declaring, "It's Time to Ignite a New Reformation!"[2] Prescient leaders, such as Greg Ogden, wrote works decades earlier including the phrase "new reformation."[3]

Despite this developing idea, October 2017 came and went with little significant change outworked in the church. Reflecting on that season, we were just too busy with the everyday operations of church life to pause and seriously consider what a

1. Downie, "Kenya Under Growing Pressure."
2. Ham, "New Reformation!"
3. Ogden, *New Reformation.*

new reformation could look like. What would it take to disrupt us from the rat wheel of ecclesiastical event management and force us to give this idea the consideration it deserved? Enter a global pandemic.

Katherine Marshall notes that pandemics have historically had an extraordinary impact on every sphere of society, including religious institutions.[4] The COVID-19 pandemic is no exception. One of the most succinct summaries of how the COVID-19 pandemic has wrought change in the church comes from Christine Caine, who writes, "The global pandemic has led to a forced pause. In the church, what we thought used to work no longer does, and perhaps we are ready to address the question of how much was really working anyway."[5] Unexpectedly, the lockdowns resulting from the COVID-19 pandemic provided the space required for us to consider this new reformation in a way that was not possible earlier. It was during a time of reflection on a family holiday that I was able to connect these dots; this new reformation was conceived in 2017 but was being birthed through the strangest of circumstances in 2020. This understanding was true for Rhythm City Church and I suspect had far-reaching relevance for the global church.

I was shocked then—though not surprised—to start hearing the concept of "reformation" being used with increasing prevalence to describe what God was doing in his church through the COVID-19 pandemic. The director of strategy for McCrindle, Grant Dusting, said that "the pandemic has left room for a 'new reformation.'"[6] Angela Williams Gorrell discusses how COVID-19 pandemic-related lockdowns might "nurture a new *reformation* in the church."[7] Brett McCracken notes the "potential for a new reformation in the digital age."[8] Arguing for a missional response from

4. Marshall, "COVID-19 and Religion," 80.
5. Caine, foreword to *ReJesus*, xv.
6. Dusting, "Re-Shaped Church."
7. Gorrell, "New Media," 59; emphasis in original.
8. McCracken, "Digital Revolution Reformation."

the church in this time, Jacques Beukes cautions that the church must "continually reform to be what it is supposed to be."[9]

Other thinkers describe the same idea using different language. Kyuboem Lee, Pieter Verster, Alfred Brunsdon, Jerry Pillay, and Beukes all describe the COVID-19 pandemic moment as an "opportunity" for change in the church.[10] Brunsdon and Pillay at times refer to this opportunity as a "Kairos moment."[11] One leading voice for the post-COVID ecclesiological era is American theologian Leonard Sweet, who interprets this opportunity as a "divine appointing and anointing" and a "'time that is given' to the church."[12] Thom Rainer writes with a heightened sense of urgency, cautioning that churches have not just an opportunity for change but a serious need for it:

> Churches don't merely have to adapt; they have to change dramatically. . . . For many years, I have advocated incremental change in churches. Most congregations are ploddingly slow to accept and then embrace change. But we no longer have the option to wait for the change-resistant to catch up. The call is truly to change or die.[13]

This statement illuminates the sacredness that this ecclesiological moment holds.

Whatever the terminology, there is a growing consensus that—despite the pain experienced worldwide—the COVID-19 pandemic was not a disaster for the church to lament, nor was it an interruption to wait out, but it was the catalyst for a significant reconfiguration of the church to reverse the present discipleship crisis. Sweet illuminates this central idea by asking a question that is both suggestive and striking: "What if the pandemic is a shock treatment which is putting the world and church back in a new

9. Beukes, "To Be," 6.

10. Lee, "COVID-19 Crisis"; Verster, "Rebuilding the Community," 9; Brunsdon, "As We Were," 8; Beukes, "To Be," 2; Pillay, "Church More Flexible," 273.

11. Brunsdon, "As We Were," 1; Pillay, "Church More Flexible," 274.

12. Sweet, "Semiotic Exegesis," 1.

13. Rainer, *Simple Church*, 18.

and better equilibrium? What if there are goldmines on the other side of the landmines and minefields?"[14] This question holds in beautiful tension both the dark reality of COVID-19's destruction, as well as the prophetic possibilities of its divine opportunity.

I believe the term *reformation* best describes both the significance and the essence of what God is doing in this new era. The word *reformation* carries the idea of a return to the blueprints of the church as found in the biblical accounts.[15] Again, Sweet proves insightful, providing a description of the post-COVID ecclesiological era that embodies this idea:

> Calamities can spur innovation. Creative disruption can stimulate new ways to innovate. However, new occurrences require new thinking, new frameworks, new metaphors, and new narratives, not that repudiate the old, but that build on the old to create something old-new, ancient-future.[16]

This idea illustrates the heart behind my call to reformation in this time, intending for it to serve as a *calling-up* for the church rather than a *calling-out* of the church, honoring what has been, while urging a reimagination of what could be.

I have also come to believe the global scale of the COVID-19 pandemic, along with the extensive scope of its ecclesiological impact, makes the word *reformation* even more apt for this event than other recent phenomena it has been used to describe. For example, the Emerging Church, Pentecostalism, and the Seeker Sensitive Church have all been described as reformations. While these movements carry reformational elements, they are largely focused on specific streams of Christian theology or practice. By contrast, in 2011 Steve Murrell referred to a "discipleship reformation," which may be prophetic for the post-COVID era and worth consideration.[17]

---

14. Sweet, "Semiotic Exegesis," 4.

15. McGrath, *Reformation Thought*, 68.

16. Sweet, "Semiotic Exegesis," 8.

17. Murrell, *WikiChurch*, 146–47.

The idea of a new reformation in the church provided me, as a church leader, the opportunity to take responsibility for my contribution to the discipleship crisis. Although frustrated by some of the responses I noticed in our congregation, I could not place the entire—or even the majority—of the blame on church members. I was starting to recognize that the insufficiencies of the ecclesiological practices I was leading were a major contributing factor to what we were observing in the response of our church members to the COVID-19 pandemic-related lockdowns.

These conclusions summarize how I answered the question "What is going on?" regarding the arrival of the COVID-19 pandemic and its implications for the church. Having obtained this clarity, I then turned my attention to the *interpretive task* in Osmer's practical theology framework, seeking to answer the question "Why is this going on?"[18] I engaged in this task with a focus on the discipleship crisis discussed above and identified two distinct, yet related, contributing factors to the situation.

18. Osmer, *Practical Theology*, 4.

4

The Interpretive Task (1)

Dependence on Weekend Services

A BARRAGE OF TEXT messages over the initial few months of lockdown indicated my good friend and I were noticing similar phenomena surrounding the impact of the COVID-19 pandemic on the church. With a long history of using each other as a theological sounding board, we made the most of a brief hiatus from lockdown restrictions to meet and discuss the situation in depth over a glass of wine. As we deliberated, one of his comments sparked a torrent of insight around the "why" behind this discipleship crisis. "I think we are seeing the result of putting too much emphasis on the Sunday service," he remarked. He was, I believe, right on point.

Rather than weekend services functioning as a jump start to propel people into fruitful Christian living Monday to Saturday, it became apparent to me that they had instead become a crutch that many church members relied on for spiritual nourishment. The arrival of COVID-19 pandemic-related lockdowns, however, had effectively kicked this spiritual crutch from underneath the church, leaving a portion of its members hobbling or unable to stand, and with no one to prop them up.[1] It was confronting to

1. Johnston et al., "Pastoral Ministry," 17.

consider that our weekend services were leaving church members spiritually infantile or ill, requiring the walking frame of the corporate gathering to stand firm. This seemed to be a stark contrast to the vision of the mature and whole body of Christ depicted in Eph 4.

Though the situation broadly reflected a dependence on the weekend service, more specifically the dependence was directed towards both the church building itself and the ministry of church leaders that was conducted in it. Concerning the former, Beukes provides an important reminder for the post-COVID era that the essence of the church is the gathering of people, not a building.[2] Although few would dispute this seemingly foundational concept, in practice I have noticed a tendency to use language around meeting *in* or *at* church rather than *as* the church. Pillay presents a similar idea, noting that although gathering is important for the church, the COVID-19 pandemic has reminded us that a building is not indispensable for that purpose.[3] A dependence on the physical building, however, was made evident by how many Christians found it challenging to gather in alternative contexts during lockdown. Despite the confronting nature of this revelation, the opportunity for reformation can be clearly seen in the midst of it. Sweet notes the paradigm-shifting capacity of the COVID-19 pandemic on how we view the church, writing, "It took a pandemic to kick the church out of its heretical notion that the ecclesia is an edifice. The confusion of the church with a building is fatal to mission, and the spell of the heresy has finally been broken."[4]

As concerning as the dependence on church buildings was, perhaps even more so was the realization of dependence on the ministry of church leaders. Shane Clifton notes one primary cause of this development, writing, "Hierarchical structures and authoritative leadership styles which generate 'dependency, helplessness, and servitude' are open to critique and change."[5] Not only was the

2. Beukes, "To Be," 2.
3. Pillay, "Church More Flexible," 268.
4. Sweet, "Semiotic Exegesis," 4.
5. Clifton, *Pentecostal Churches in Transition*, 209.

COVID-19 pandemic revealing the presence of such hierarchical leadership structures and outcomes, but it was also providing the very context for such a critique of them. Pillay writes that COVID-19

> has "flattened the curve" on hierarchical church structures. It has shown us that faith survives without pastors, priests, and bishops. The closure of churches has led to the reinforcement of the "priest" in each home; someone in the home takes the lead to provide spiritual guidance and nurturance for the family.[6]

Sadly, this overemphasis on the giftedness and calling of church leaders has been a recurring theme throughout various epochs of church history. For example, Derek Tidball records the appearance of hierarchical leadership approaches as early as the second century.[7] Reducing the clergy-laity divide undergirded much of what took place in the Protestant Reformation in the 1500s.[8] Australian Pentecostalism, although starting out with free-church leadership structures in the early 1900s, gradually morphed into more hierarchical models throughout its history.[9] CEO models of leadership in the modern day are prone to the same pattern.[10] Now in the post-COVID era—and much to my surprise—some Rhythm City Church members were showing signs of dependence on the ministry of church leaders for spiritual vitality, pointing towards a lack of empowerment of every church member.

6. Pillay, "Church More Flexible," 272.

7. Tidball, *Skilful Shepherds*, 148–49.

8. McGrath, *Reformation Thought*, 111–12.

9. Austin et al., *Asia Pacific Pentecostalism*, 391.

10. Fitch, *Great Giveaway*, 82.

5

The Interpretive Task (2)

Consumer Christianity

WHILE IT WAS EVIDENT that dependence on weekend services was a significant factor in the church's discipleship crisis, I noticed a more intricate web of underlying influences. This insight did not emerge from a singular event or conversation; instead, it crystallized over time as I connected the dots between the discipleship crisis and what has come to be known as "consumer Christianity." Although I was aware of this phenomenon prior to the COVID-19 pandemic, this exercise in practical theology heightened my understanding of its detrimental impact on the discipleship task. A deeper understanding of two other phenomena—consumerism and the attractional church—serve to illuminate this connection.

To understand *consumerism*, it is important to differentiate between consumerism and consumption. While consumption is part of what it means to be human, how we consume has ethical implications. Laura Hartman provides helpful insight into this, contending that good Christian consumption is fourfold: (1) it avoids sin, (2) it embraces creation, (3) it loves the neighbor, and (4) it envisions the future.[1] In a similar manner,

---

1. Hartman, *Christian Consumer*, 20.

Craig Bartholomew distinguishes between consumerism and commerce, arguing, "It is possible to see commercial develop-ment within culture as healthy while seeing consumerism as an unhealthy development of commerce."[2]

Consumerism, then, is an ethos that promotes excessive hab-its of consumption as the key driver of economic growth, often in ways that are at odds with biblical ideas such as contentment and environmental stewardship.[3] It has complex origins and has evolved over several centuries, but one major catalyst of its contem-porary form was the Industrial Revolution.[4] Kerryn Higgs notes that while consumption was historically driven by subsistence, the means for mass production created by the Industrial Revolution shifted the focus toward wants and desires, making them the driv-ing force for a wider segment of the industrialized world.[5]

By the 1920s, overproduction became a resulting economic issue, with Edward Bernays noting in 1928, "Mass production is profitable only if its rhythm can be maintained—that is if it can continue to sell its product in steady or increasing quantity."[6] In an attempt to keep demand greater than supply, tools such as adver-tising were employed to create a repeating cycle of desire for, and discontentment with, new products and services.[7] Although mass consumption slowed during the Great Depression of the 1930s and World War II, the post-war economic boom of the 1950s provided the environment for consumerism to resume its acceleration. Vic-tor Lebow captured this evolving ethos in 1955, stating,

> Our enormously productive economy demands that we make consumption our way of life, that we con-vert the buying and use of goods into rituals, that we seek our spiritual satisfaction, our ego satisfaction, in

2. Bartholomew, "Christ and Consumerism," 6.

3. Wilk, "Consumption," 5.

4. Bartholomew, "Christ and Consumerism," 4.

5. Higgs, "Brief History."

6. Bernays, *Propaganda*, 63.

7. Hartman, *Christian Consumer*, 14.

16

consumption. . . . We need things consumed, burned up, replaced and discarded at an ever-accelerating rate.[8]

It was in the environment of the 1960s to 1980s—a time of further intensification for consumerism—that the contemporary evangelical church was born and shaped. A new generation of church leaders emerged, seeking to leverage elements of this culture for kingdom purposes, aiming to rescue the church from irrelevance in a time of decline and to lead masses to faith in Christ. One significant expression of this effort was the seeker-sensitive church, a model pioneered by Bill Hybels of Willow Creek Community Church, Rick Warren of Saddleback Valley Community Church, and even earlier, Robert Schuller of Crystal Cathedral.[9] The seeker-sensitive movement has since morphed into a diverse array of churches that share a similar methodological foundation. Jared C. Wilson categorizes this model as the *attractional church* and aptly describes the essence of its philosophy as follows:

> A definition of "attractional" would perhaps be something like this: a way of ministry that derives from the primary purpose of making Christianity appealing. By this definition, it would not be an exaggeration to say that the attractional church makes its primary aim in worship to get as many people through the doors of the church as possible so that they may hear what it means to have a relationship with Jesus Christ.[10]

Attractional philosophies have been widely adopted across various streams of Christianity since its origin. In reflecting on their impact over the past several decades, it became apparent to me that the fathers and mothers who pioneered the attractional model did so largely with benevolent and noble aspirations. Although reformation requires a critique of ideas, it is important we do not criticize the people who tried to pave a way for those to come, often at personal cost. Still, a critique is required as, despite

8. Higgs, "Brief History."
9. Wilson, *Prodigal Church*, 22; Stafford, "Died."
10. Wilson, *Prodigal Church*, 22.

the best of intentions, the attractional model seems to have been weighed and found wanting. That is not to say that churches who adhere to an attractional model are rotten to the core and those who do not are without blemish. God is at work in his church, as imperfect as we all are, and good fruit comes even through broken vessels. Still, it must be acknowledged that the attractional model has contributed to the discipleship crisis we are now experiencing, and if we are to walk into healthier ecclesiological expressions, these shortcomings must be identified and addressed.

The attractional model appears to have fallen short of its intended purpose in six ways. Firstly, it has led to the church being identified as a business. A vigorous push towards this identity can be seen at least as early as 1912 with Shailer Mathews, dean of the University of Chicago Divinity School.[11] Andrew J. Ball summarizes Mathews's key ideas, writing, "Mathews claimed that if the church was to survive in the age of business, it must begin to conceive of itself as a business enterprise, adopting the methods, mores, and rationalized modes of organization prevailing in the industrial and commercial sectors."[12] Similar ideas continued to gain momentum throughout the twentieth-century, reaching their zenith in the 1980s and 1990s as voices like George Barna suggested the future success of the church would depend on marketing models originating in the business world.[13]

Today, the business world has had such a profound impact that it would be difficult to find a church that is not structured around the four functional areas of business—namely, (1) marketing, (2) operations, (3) finance, and (4) human resources; all under the umbrella of strategic management.[14] Interpreting this church-business relationship remains complex, however, in that there are both benefits and disadvantages for the church in adopting ideas and practices from the business world. The functional area of finance, for example, includes important implications for both the

11. Mathews, *Scientific Management*.

12. Ball, "Christianity Incorporated," 81.

13. Wells, *God in the Wasteland*, loc. 871.

14. Jiang, "Strategic Management," 153.

sustainability of ministry activities in the congregation and discipleship growth in the individual.[15] For some financial aspects, there is merit—and even necessity—in gleaning insight from the corporate world. When profits and paychecks become the motivation behind ministry decisions, however, business philosophies have replaced biblical faithfulness as the priority of the church.

Drawing insights from the business world can be valuable, but conflating the church with business rather than identifying with the biblical motifs of family, body, and temple as noted in Eph 2:19–22 has, in my view, a harmful effect on the church's commission to make disciples.[16] It is the negative outcomes that led Robert Farrar Capon to describe the church-business conglomeration as "the worst thing that ever happened to the church."[17] Eugene Peterson describes his conclusion of the attractional theories he was being taught with more potent language:

> After a few years of trying to take all of this seriously, I decided that I was being lied to. This is the Americanization of congregation. It means turning each congregation into a market for religious consumers, an ecclesiastical business run along the lines of advertising techniques and organizational flow charts, and then energized by impressive motivational rhetoric. . . . The pragmatic vocational embrace of American technology and consumerism that promised to rescue congregations from ineffective obscurity violated everything—scriptural, theological, experiential—that formed my identity as a follower of Jesus. It struck me as a terrible desecration of a way of life to which the church had ordained me, something on the order of a vocational abomination of desolation.[18]

The perceived benefits of business philosophies can make it seem overly critical and even absurd to describe them in such

15. Fitch, *Great Giveaway*, 27; Malphurs and Stoope, *Money Matters in Church*, 15.

16. Stott, *Message of Ephesians*, 24.

17. Farrar Capon, *Astonished Heart*, 79.

18. Peterson, *Pastor*, 143.

terms. Further, few attractional leaders would theorize that the church is *only* a business. Yet, an honest look at the adverse outcomes of business paradigms for discipleship, considering the COVID-19 pandemic response, has led me to a similarly disparaging assessment rather than tolerating them as an unfortunate but necessary counterpart to the benefits.

With the church identified as a business, the second drift of the attractional model was to become preoccupied with providing a product. Where the motivation is most benevolent, salvation is what attractional church proponents are trying to help people acquire. Kimon Sargeant—an advocate for the attractional model—describes the distinguishing characteristic of the movement as designing "services, programs, messages, and ministries that will appeal to unchurched individuals. By changing the form in which Sunday messages are delivered, seeker churches offer religious consumers a product that might not have been inviting in its traditional packaging."[19] The captivation with getting people to attend a gathering to do so, however, unwittingly leads to the packaging becoming a product. In this case, the product became weekend services, as well as any number of other programs or services sanctioned by the church. Whether intentionally or inadvertently, this approach sends a strong message to the community that God is only accessible at official church gatherings.[20] Is it any wonder we were left with a large portion of church members during the COVID-19 pandemic that was dependent on weekend services and the ministry of church leaders?

Third, not only do attractional churches tend towards fixation on the product of church services and programs, but those very gathering points can become customer-centered rather than Christ-centered. Lyle E. Schaller identifies Theodore Levitt as the catalytic voice that shifted business methodologies from being producer-focused to the consumer-driven approach we see prevalent today, even in the church.[21] We can see the philosophy's

19. Sargeant, *Seeker Churches*, loc. 118.
20. Frost and Hirsch, *Shaping of Things*, 41.
21. Schaller, *New Reformation*, 71.

ecclesiological influence in the quote Bill Hybels had hanging outside his office from management guru Peter Drucker, which read, "What is our business? Who is our customer? What does the customer consider value?"[22]

Two problems become evident upon consideration of this approach. To begin, Wilson notes that "very often, what the customer wants is *not* what the customer needs."[23] In other words, what a person wants is not always compatible with the walk of discipleship. For example, I recall being taught the importance of having an excellent children's ministry in Bible college, as many parents would choose a church based on this factor alone. Now, as both a pastor and a father, I see this as a fickle way to discover spiritual family and believe the onus is on parents to disciple their children into the church that they sense God is leading them to. Further, what a church perceives the "customer" wants is not always accurate. Craig Groeschel, for example, at one point realized he needed to preach deeper content in his quest to reach unbelievers than he first thought appropriate based on new information about questions they were asking.[24] Discipleship—and leadership for that matter—often involves providing people with what they need before they know they need it. Meeting needs—whether genuine or felt—may be a primary objective of business, but it is not the priority of the church.[25]

Fourth, with a commitment to provide customers with a product they perceive is needed, it is a logical progression for attractional churches to encourage evangelistic strategies based more on marketing than missional living. This is not surprising, considering both the program-focused nature of attractional churches along with the fact that many thought leaders in the business world see marketing as primary among the key functional business areas.[26]

22. Drucker, "Trusting the Teacher."

23. Wilson, *Gospel-Driven Church*, 26; emphasis in original.

24. Wilson, *Gospel-Driven Church*, 31.

25. For a comprehensive critique of meeting needs in the church, see Wells, *God in the Wasteland*.

26. Jiang, "Strategic Management," 153.

This is significantly detrimental to the discipleship task, reducing evangelism to "come and see" strategies that require Christians to bring unbelievers to professional clergy to connect with God.[27] Few strategies have disempowered disciples of Jesus to make other disciples over the past few decades more than the oversimplified admonition of church leaders to "invite and bring" people to church.

Another feature of marketing is that it enables organizations to stand out among their competitors.[28] If salvation remained the product, and non-Christians were therefore seen as the customers, it would logically follow that the competitor for an attractional church would be various religions, philosophies, and worldviews vying for worship and adherence. Since the product has become weekend services and programs, however, other Christians have replaced non-Christians as customers, and other churches who offer similar products are now viewed as competitors.[29] This marks the fifth area of departure in the attractional model. To remain a viable option amid growing competition, churches must continually enhance their programs, create compelling vision statements, and avoid speaking truths that might bring discomfort to such a level that members might consider an alternative brand. None of this is conducive to healthy discipleship outcomes.

Finally, one of the most damaging outcomes of the corporate influence on attractional models is the measuring of success using business standards rather than biblical ones. Primarily, this is done using numerical metrics around church attendance, salvation decisions, and financial giving.[30] In business terms, these may relate to customer retention, customer acquisition, and profit margin.[31] An excessive focus on these areas can have negative consequences for discipleship, observing outcomes that may not be a measure

27. Frost and Hirsch, *Shaping of Things*, 41.

28. Suidan Al Badi, "Impact of Marketing Mix," 8.

29. Schaller, *New Reformation*, 122–23; Wilson, *Prodigal Church*, 30–31.

30. McKnight and McKnight Barringer, *Church Called Tov*, 204; Fitch, *Great Giveaway*, 31.

31. Stahl et al., "Impact of Brand Equity."

of health, and omitting ones that are important.[32] In his balanced critique of using numerical metrics in the church, David E. Fitch pinpoints the major problem in this area, writing, "Perhaps most disturbing is the way we evangelicals are attracted to big numbers. It goes with the evangelical territory that the biggest churches get the attention, the acclamation of success."[33] It was this very obsession with "bigness" that caused Donald McGavran—founder of the Church Growth movement—to resist having Church Growth principles taught in North America.[34] Gary McIntosh points out that McGavran feared the American fondness for bigness would turn what was originally a vision for evangelism through cross-cultural church planting into something corporate and entrepreneurial.[35] It seems that which McGavran feared came upon him and that it was "church growth gone wrong," not McGavran or his founding philosophies, that added fuel to the fire of attractional methodologies.

This deviation from the intended trajectory of the attractional model resulted not in the mass formation of disciples but in a fusion of Christianity with consumer capitalism—a form of syncretism now commonly referred to as *consumer Christianity*. Numerous symptoms of consumer Christianity appear to be fundamentally at odds with the walk of discipleship, and although it is beyond the scope of this work, a thorough exploration of these would be a beneficial endeavor for church leaders and their teams. What alarms me most is the way a consumer mentality perverts the kind of love Jesus calls his followers to show—both toward God and toward one another.

In our relationship with God, consumer Christianity reduces him to a genie rather than recognizing him as our Holy Father. While both a genie and a father may be generous, a genie exists solely to fulfill the wishes of its less powerful but more commanding master. Viewing God in this way fosters a self-centered approach to the relationship, undermining the kind of love Jesus said

32. Wilson, *Gospel-Driven Church*, 41–47.
33. Fitch, *Great Giveaway*, 28.
34. Vaters, "Unexpected Origins."
35. Vaters, "Unexpected Origins."

should be the highest priority for God's people (Matt 22:37–38). A Holy Father, on the other hand, invites us into a loving relationship marked by reverence, trust, and surrender. David Wells articulates this idea aptly:

> We have turned to a God that we can use rather than to a God we must obey; we have turned to a God who will fulfill our needs rather than to a God before whom we must surrender our rights to ourselves. He is a God for us, for our satisfaction—not because we have learned to think of him in this way through Christ but because we have learned to think of him this way through the marketplace. . . . And so we transform the God of mercy into a God who is at our mercy.[36]

This view does serious damage to the beauty and richness God intends for our relationship with him. It neglects the mysterious tension between his transcendence and omniscience and the invitation on offer to know him intimately.

No less damaging is the influence of consumer Christianity on our relationships with one another. In his discourse surrounding the Last Supper—recorded in John 13–17—Jesus offers a compelling vision of the priority God places on these relationships. While love for all people is central to the Christian life (cf. Matt 22:39), the Johannine narrative highlights the distinct kingdom impact that flows from love among believers. Notably, Jesus teaches that the defining mark of his disciples is their love for one another (John 13:35). While the implications of this are felt across the universal church, it is the local church where this love finds concrete expression.[37] Unfortunately, this vision for the local church has been corrupted by the influence of consumer Christianity.

The explosion of church shopping and church hopping has become one of the most telling expressions of consumer Christianity within the local church. Searching for a new church is sometimes necessary—such as during times of geographical relocation and when facing irreconcilable theological or philosophical

36. Wells, *God in the Wasteland*, loc. 1403.
37. Grenz, *Theology for the Community*, 467–68.

differences—but the purpose should always be to find a community where you can plant roots and participate fully in its life. Ideally, the journey involves discerning shared values and committing to meaningful relationships. The consumer-minded Christian, however, often approaches this search through the lens of personal preference and felt needs.

Local churches do, in fact, meet a variety of genuine human needs, and members rightly consume legitimate resources such as the sacraments, the Scriptures, and mutual encouragement. But felt needs are often fleeting and subjective, constantly shifting with the individual's circumstances and desires. When people are given permission to define their needs entirely on their own terms, the result is often a transition from seasons of church shopping to cycles of church hopping. As Wells observes,

> Allowing the consumer to be sovereign in this way in fact sanctions a bad habit. It encourages us to indulge in constant internal inventory in the church no less than in the marketplace, to ask ourselves perpetually whether the "products" we are being offered meet our present "felt needs." In this sort of environment, market research has found that there is scarcely any consumer loyalty to particular products and brands anymore. The consumer, like the marketeer, is now making fresh calculations all the time. And so it is that the churches that have adopted the strategy of marketing themselves have effectively installed revolving doors. The pews may be full, but never with the same people from week to week. People keep entering, lured by the church's attractions or just to check out the wares, but then they move on because they feel their needs, real or otherwise, are not being met.[38]

Some of the underlying causes of church hopping do not ultimately arise from church practices, but from the heart—an issue that accompanies the individual from one church to the next. The tendency of consumer Christianity to place the self at the center of spirituality leads to a range of distortions in the understanding of church—such as sporadic attendance, dismissing the importance

38. Wells, *God in the Wasteland*, loc. 902.

of gathering altogether, and adopting a passive, spectator mindset rather than actively engaging in the life of the church community. These patterns are incompatible with the mark of Christlike love that, according to Jesus, defines the journey of discipleship.[39]

Despite the best of intentions, the attractional church and it's resulting consumer Christianity have proved limited in helping people start a journey of discipleship, and even more inept at maturing them throughout the process.[40] It has reduced Christianity to *Churchianity*, allowing the consumption of church services to replace obedience to God.[41] With these influences dominant, is it any wonder that, during the COVID-19 pandemic, church leaders realized there were more people in the pews than they would like to admit who were governed more by principles of consumerism than embodying the life of discipleship laid out in Scripture? These understandings were a serious wake-up call for me. They forced me to stop blaming congregation members and external factors for the presence of consumerism in my church and to take responsibility for creating the structures designed to produce it. Although we did not arrive at this place intentionally, I realized that what we say we value at Rhythm City Church is futile if our practices are not aligned with those values.[42] I have come to view consumer Christianity not as a flawed yet salvageable expression of Christianity, but as an outdated distortion of the faith that we must allow God to detox from the body of Christ.

39. For a thorough exploration on the church as a covenant people, see Grenz, *Theology for the Community*, 464–72.

40. Wilson, *Prodigal Church*, 22–40.

41. Willard, *Great Omission*, 52.

42. Frost and Hirsch, *Shaping of Things*, 68–69.

6

The Normative Task (1)

Disciple-Making Churches

AFTER LABORING WITH GOD through the descriptive-empirical and interpretive tasks, I naturally progressed to Osmer's third task of practical theology—*the normative task*—wherein I addressed the question "What ought to be happening?"[1] This step was less complex than the first two, with the answer immediately apparent. If we were experiencing a discipleship crisis due to church models that created dependency within God's people, then we should have been—and therefore need to become—a disciple-making church that equips God's people to live what I have come to call a self-initiated spirituality. Bill Hull highlights the call for a discipleship focus within the church, writing, "I believe the discipling church is the normal church and that disciple-making is for everyone and every church."[2]

Several ecclesiological theories have come to underpin my understanding of the importance of building *disciple-making churches*. Firstly, as I considered this fresh insight, it renewed my strength of conviction that making disciples is the key mission

1. Osmer, *Practical Theology*, 4.
2. Hull, *Disciple-Making Church*, 17.

given to every church in every age (Matt 28:10–20). This is an idea also asserted by voices such as Hugh Halter and Matt Smay, Philip Graham Ryken, and Aubrey Malphurs.[3] Although my wife and I had previously aligned our mission statement with the Great Commission when planting the Nairobi church, it ultimately remained an idea written on vision documents without permeating the culture of the church. Not only did the idea not carry conviction at that time, but upon reflection I can see that attractional warnings deterred me from leading too strongly towards discipleship truths for fear of people not being able to handle it. Now, in this new era, I could not help but imagine what it would look like if every church—rather than creating vision and mission statements that tried to distinguish themselves from other churches—unapologetically aligned with others in the shared mission of disciple-making.

That is not to suggest that there are no distinguishing elements among churches. Every church, for example, is unique in what Frank Damazio calls *metron*, based on the use of the word in 2 Cor 10:13. Metron, Damazio writes, "is an assigned scope of ministry grace and ministry influence within the limits of appointed lines drawn by God."[4] Differences in metron could include the various gift sets possessed by church leaders, variations between mono-site and multi-site models, and geographical diversity. It may be necessary to help congregations understand some of these dynamics, but a unique metron should not be emphasized above the universal mission of every church to make disciples.

Another important idea guiding the priority of disciple-making is that discipleship is not an optional extra reserved for church leaders or serious Christians. This idea has been one of Dallas Willard's major contributions to the church over the last few decades, one that has been echoed by authors such as Greg Ogden and Bill Hull.[5] Willard illuminates a prevalent ecclesiological error, writing,

---

3. Halter and Smay, *AND*, 89; Ryken, *City on a Hill*, 139; Malphurs, *Advanced Strategic Planning*, 113–14.

4. Damazio, *Life Changing Leadership*, 20.

5. Willard, *Great Omission*, 4; Ogden, *Transforming Discipleship*, 49; Hull, *Disciple-Making Church*, 24.

> For at least several decades the churches of the Western world have not made discipleship a condition of being a Christian. One is not required to be, or to intend to be, a disciple in order to become a Christian, and one may remain a Christian without any signs of progress toward or in discipleship. . . . So far as the visible Christian institutions of our day are concerned, *discipleship is clearly optional.*[6]

Willard and many others have effectively refuted this idea as biblically unfaithful, rebutting that discipleship is not a separate level of Christianity but is inseparable from it and even synonymous with it.[7] Rather than being an optional extra—leather seats that can be either selected or omitted in favor of the base model—discipleship is the very essence of what it means to be Christian.

Further, discipleship cannot be reduced to one ecclesiological theory or a singular stream of Christianity. The most common reductionist view of discipleship is to equate it with spiritual formation. One author, for example, writes, "Not to mention, it seems that discipleship (formation) seems to be of minimal importance in many churches when compared to evangelism and church growth strategies."[8] While it is an important element of discipleship, formation is not the same as discipleship.[9] Another tendency is to view discipleship as one of many ecclesiological flavors within Christianity. Richard Foster, for example, notes six different streams of Christianity, including the charismatic and contemplative streams.[10] While each of these makes a unique contribution to the discipleship task, discipleship cannot be minimized to stream number seven. On the contrary, its universal nature has led me to view discipleship as an ecumenical umbrella encompassing the diverse expressions within the Christian faith. This perspective emphasizes the significance of discipleship in the Christian journey,

6. Willard, *Great Omission*, 4; emphasis in original.

7. Ogden, *Transforming Discipleship*, 49; Hull, *Disciple-Making Church*, 24.

8. Davis, *Trinitarian Formation*, xix.

9. See also appendix 3 of this book: "Discipleship and Spiritual Formation."

10. Foster, *Streams of Living Water*.

in turn eliminating the temptation to omit it from ecclesiological theory and practice.

Finally, discipleship-focused ecclesiological models provide a biblical alternative to the destructive attractional models discussed under the interpretive task. Jim Putman and Bobby Harrington make a case for this, noting that their book *DiscipleShift* espouses a *relational-discipleship* model of church, an alternative to the attractional paradigms they had shifted from in their own ministry practice.[11] Alan Hirsch adds to the idea, noting that discipleship is the opposing force to the consumerism that results from attractional models.[12] This suggestion is a slight departure from purely missional church proponents, who often promote missional models as the antithesis of attractional ones.[13] Although missional theorists hold valuable insights for biblical discipleship, discipleship models hold more holistic strategies for health than missional living alone.

As these insights consolidated, a slight trepidation surfaced within me. I thought, "What if no one at Rhythm City Church is ready for a bold, intentional shift toward discipleship—and they all decide to walk away? With two young daughters now, what if that affects church finances to the point that they are unable to sustain our salary?" As I considered this, I made an internal commitment before the Lord that I would lead in this season of ministry out of obedience to the mission of making disciples, not to preserve a paycheck—even if that meant finding employment elsewhere as we worked towards reforming the church.

11. Putman and Harrington, *DiscipleShift*, 16.
12. Hirsch, *Forgotten Ways*, 112.
13. Frost, "Coronavirus."

7

The Normative Task (2)
Self-Initiated Spirituality

As THE LOCKDOWN STRATEGY was discontinued in Australia and international travel opened, we gathered the teams from both Nairobi and Newcastle for a leadership retreat in Dubai. Not only was this the first time the two groups had met face-to-face, but the gathering provided an opportunity for us to process some of the key insights we had been discussing about the post-COVID church. One item on the agenda was to create a statement to help our church members—as well as those who would join in the future—understand the essence of what God had deposited in us through this COVID-19 phenomenon. It was here that we created the Rhythm City Church heartbeat statement, an attempt to communicate the ideas that defined us in less corporate terms than a vision and mission statement.

The statement that emerged read, "The Heartbeat of Rhythm City Church is to be a global family of maturing, Spirit-filled followers of Jesus." The first half encapsulated our desire at that time to develop a multi-site church with locations in three countries around the world—with Dubai to be added in the future—and evoked little difference of opinion among the team. The second half communicated our conviction around the centrality of disciple-making to the mission of the church, with "Spirit-filled" and "maturing" chosen to describe the non-negotiable values we wanted to see underpinning our disciple-making.

The "Spirit-filled" descriptor stirred some level of discussion among the team. No one questioned whether the empowerment of the Holy Spirit was core to the heartbeat of the church, but some team members felt a phrase like "Spirit-led" would minimize potential misunderstandings resulting from unhealthy expressions of Pentecostalism. One team member contested this idea, contending passionately that "Spirit-led" could be used within any stream of Christianity and that nothing less than "Spirit-filled" would adequately convey this value. This resonated deeply with me as, over the previous two decades, I had noticed a concerning trend described succinctly by Angelo Cettolin. He writes, "More recently, however, some Pentecostal and Charismatic movements are playing down features of historic or classical Pentecostalism and moving towards more traditional or mainline expressions of the Christian life in their practices and beliefs."[1] "Spirit-filled" was subsequently chosen to resist such a trend in Rhythm City Church and to represent our unapologetic alignment with Pentecostalism.

The word "maturing" was, however, the most debated. It morphed from our initial selection, "mature," to avoid making us sound pretentious and "perfected." It was then almost scrapped completely, as some young people in our team were concerned it sounded boring. Ultimately, we kept it, as "maturity" was one of the major themes that kept surfacing in our community regarding discipleship over the COVID-19 pandemic season. This is an idea shared by Aubrey Malphurs, who identifies the direction of the church as "making mature disciples."[2] A second conviction that formed during this normative task, therefore, was the idea of a *self-initiated spirituality*, a characteristic we have come to view as central to mature discipleship. The idea is that as a disciple progresses in their spiritual journey, they should become less dependent

1. Cettolin, *Spirit Freedom and Power*, loc. 44.
2. Malphurs, *Strategic Disciple Making*, 10.

on external factors—such as weekend services and church leaders—for motivation to live a fruitful and vibrant spiritual life. We borrowed the word "self-initiating" from Greg Ogden, after our Nairobi team suggested the initial choice—*self-governed spirituality*—was too reflective of unaccountable, autocratic political leadership models in their context.[3]

Johnston, Eagle, Headley, and Holleman report that other church leaders have highlighted this as an important concept emerging from the COVID-19 pandemic, writing,

> The practical realities of COVID-19 created circumstances in which congregants could no longer depend on the pastor and/or on weekly services as the main pillars of their faith life. Instead, the pandemic forced congregants, as Christian put it, to "pick up a spoon" and become more agentic in their spiritual growth—rather than be "spoon-fed" by pastors.[4]

Several church leaders have referred to this concept as "self-feeding."[5] Famously, Bill Hybels admitted mistakes he made in creating the Willow Creek seeker-sensitive church model, saying they should have instead been teaching people to become "self-feeders."[6] Wilson encourages caution around this phrase, however, noting it can absolve church leadership from their responsibilities by overemphasizing the role of the individual.[7] Darrin Patrick makes similar observations, encouraging a balance between "spoon-feeding" and "self-feeding."[8]

"Self-initiating" seems to effectively sum up the idea, referring more to the source or motivation of the discipleship impetus than to discipleship behaviors. On one hand, it shifts the focus of the church's responsibility rather than absolving it, emphasizing the importance of *equipping* rather than *feeding* God's people—an

3. Ogden, *Transforming Discipleship*, 55.

4. Johnston et al., "Pastoral Ministry," 17.

5. E.g., Cordeiro, *Irresistible Church*, loc. 89; Frost, "Coronavirus."

6. Wilson, *Prodigal Church*, 124.

7. Wilson, *Prodigal Church*, 124–25.

8. Patrick, "Control Tweaks."

idea importantly expanded by Ogden.[9] On the other, it recognizes the inner catalyst required for driving spiritual practices, one that must become autonomous for maturity to take place. In an age where many Christians find it difficult to rise above both the apathy that comes with life's comforts and the anxiety that comes with its challenges, I have come to see self-initiation as a vital skill for mature discipleship.

9. Ogden, *New Reformation*, 109.

8

The Pragmatic Task (1)

Four Goals of Discipleship

THE QUESTION "HOW MIGHT we respond?" encapsulates Osmer's fourth task of practical theology, *the pragmatic task.* Put in context, I asked, "How do I create a disciple-making church that equips individuals to self-initiate their Christian walk?" Not only did this question guide my initial post-COVID leadership response, but it continues to shape what I now anticipate will be a life-long journey of discovering best practices for mobilizing discipleship in the church.

It did not take long for me to identify the starting point for this task to be developing a definition of discipleship. As I explored this task, I discovered that I was not alone in this pursuit. For decades, numerous voices have drawn attention to the urgent need for greater clarity around what discipleship means. In his theological work on discipleship, J. Chase Davis argues that discipleship has been insufficiently defined within the Evangelical church.[1] Similarly, Bill Hull identifies the lack of a shared definition as a major obstacle, asserting that discussions around discipleship are

1. Davis, *Trinitarian Formation*, xix.

futile without it.[2] This concern is echoed in *The State of Disciple-ship*, a research project by the Barna Group commissioned by the Navigators. The executive summary captures the issue succinctly:

> A critical component of this study is to *define* "disciple-ship." The concept is familiar to many, but a widely accepted definition remains elusive. Although it may seem a mere technicality, accurate and relevant termi-nology and a clear definition are important first steps toward ensuring a church or ministry can effectively grow disciples.[3]

As I continued my research, it became increasingly evident that this lack of definition has hindered the intentionality needed for churches to make disciples in a meaningful and effective way.

Several factors appear to have contributed to this lack of definitional clarity. In my view, the most significant one is that discipleship is not mono-faceted; rather, it is a complex phenom-enon with many constituent elements.[4] A comprehensive defining of discipleship could involve any of its key dimensions—the who, what, when, where, how, or why. For example, the stages of dis-cipleship could be defined; this is something that Dann Spader, Jim Putman, and Don Willett have contributed towards in their respective works. Spader identifies the different stages of growth in the discipleship journey as (1) seekers, (2) believers, (3) workers, and (4) reproducers.[5] Putman defines the stages along different lines, listing them as (1) spiritually dead, (2) spiritual infant, (3) spiritual child, (4) spiritual young adult, and (5) spiritual parent.[6] Willett interprets 1 John 2:12–14 to identify three stages: (1) chil-dren, (2) young adults, and (3) mature fathers.[7]

The environments of discipleship could also be the target of definition, exploring the contexts in which discipleship takes

2. Hull, *Conversion and Discipleship*, 22.
3. Barna Group, *State of Discipleship*, 9.
4. Hayes and Cherry, *Meanings of Discipleship*, 234–35.
5. Spader, *4 Chair Discipling*, 60.
6. Putman, *Real-Life Discipleship*, 43.
7. Willett, "Biblical Model," 92.

place. Harrington and Absalom suggest five contexts of discipleship: (1) public (one hundred or more people); (2) social (twenty
to seventy people); (3) personal (four to twelve people); transpar-
ent (one to two people); and (5) divine (disciple and God).[8] J. T.
English presents a case for various educational contexts, while also
crediting value to Sunday services and small groups.[9] There are
several other ways that discipleship could be defined, including
an examination of the etymology of *discipleship*, or in terms of the
processes and tools of discipleship.

In considering the possibilities, I concluded that the single
most important task was to define the goals of discipleship. The
goals of discipleship, as I intend and understand the phrase, refers
to the outcomes one desires to see produced in the lives of those
who follow Jesus. Ken Adams summarizes my rationale for this
aptly, writing, "First, define what it looks like when a disciple has
been made! Think about it. What good is it to have a plan for making disciples if you don't know what kind of disciples you are seeking to make."[10] Ron Bennett provokes similar thinking, asking, "If
a person gets involved in a disciple making ministry, what kind
of change do you anticipate seeing in that person in the next five
years?"[11] Understanding the end goals of discipleship is essential
for determining the appropriate programs and systems required to
see them embodied in people's lives.

A further observation emerged in defining the goals of discipleship: any definition must be broad enough to capture the full
scope of the discipleship journey, yet concrete enough to help
practitioners create a plan for making disciples. It is important
to resist the tendency to provide definitions in terms that are
either too expansive or too narrow. A simple online search or a
brief survey of existing literature, for example, will reveal the
commonly proposed idea that the singular goal of discipleship is

---

8. Harrington and Absalom, *Discipleship That Fits*, 33–35.

9. English, *Deep Discipleship*, 87–91.

10. Adams, "Two Questions."

11. Bennett, *Intentional Disciplemaking*, loc. 188.

37

Christlikeness.[12] While this sentiment is theologically sound—and often an important warning against program driven approaches—its vagueness offers little practical guidance for those tasked with making disciples.

Conversely, when definitions become too specific, they often shift focus from the actual goals of discipleship to the practices that help achieve those goals. A common example I have come across is prayer. While prayer is essential, it is not a goal of discipleship itself, but rather a vital practice in pursuing the deeper aim—intimate knowledge of God. Overly detailed definitions risk losing the outlook needed to capture the full scope of what discipleship truly seeks to accomplish.

After much contemplation, four goals became apparent as being broad enough, yet specific enough, to encompass the various fruit produced in a disciple's life. Consequently, I introduced the goals of discipleship to the Rhythm City Church community as: (1) *enjoying a relationship with God*, (2) *embodying the image of God*, (3) *embracing the family of God*, and (4) *engaging the mission of God*. In consultation with our church leadership teams, I continue to experiment with the precise terminology of these goals to ensure communicative clarity within the congregation, but the terms' essence remains unchanged.

A relationship with God is an essential starting point. As Robert Gallaty notes, "The discipleship process always begins here, with a personal relationship with Jesus."[13] A call to spiritual growth is reflected in the image of God goal, referred to throughout Christian literature in terms like spiritual formation, transformation, and sanctification. This goal is so crucial to the discipleship task that it has at times—erroneously, in my view—been equated with it. As previously noted, to reflect the image of Christ plays a significant role in the discipleship journey, but it does not fully define it. Being immersed in the family of God refers to how one participates in the church, the community of faith inseparable from one's

12. For example, see Frost and Hirsch, *ReJesus*, xviii.
13. Gallaty, *Rediscovering Discipleship*, 47.

THE PRAGMATIC TASK (1)

salvation.[14] The fourth and final goal relates to partnering with God's mission in the world, a task Alan Hirsch calls an "essential task of discipleship."[15]

These four goals of discipleship were developed through two key influences. Firstly, their biblical foundation is drawn from the account of the first disciples being called in the opening chapter of the Gospel of John. In that story, Jesus calls Andrew and another disciple to follow him, revealing a relationship with God to be central to the discipleship journey. The importance of a disciple becoming more like Christ can be observed by Jesus changing Simon's name to Peter, a prophetic picture of Peter's future transformation. Following Jesus in this account entailed doing so in the context of a community, indicating discipleship is a collective, familial—rather than solitary—experience. Finally, most of the disciples called to follow Jesus in this narrative ended up searching for others to bring on the same journey, participating with Jesus in spreading the gospel. An example of this is Andrew going to find Simon to bring him to Jesus.

Secondly, from a theological perspective, ideas from Trinitarian theology were influential, particularly those of Michael Reeves and Fred Sanders. Prior to engaging their works, I had already begun to draw connections between the four goals of discipleship and the notion of abiding in the love of the Trinity. I imagined that as a disciple abides in this divine love, the four goals accurately describe what would naturally emerge: intimate relationship with God, transformation into the image of Christ, communion with others who have been brought into that love, and an outworking of the love received into the world. Reeves vividly describes this dynamic of our union with Christ, writing, "The God who loves to have an outgoing Image of himself in his Son loves to have many images of his love (who are themselves outgoing)."[16] This captured the very ideas I had been contemplating.

---

14. Geiger et al., *Transformational Discipleship*, 172.

15. Hirsch, *Forgotten Ways*, 110.

16. Reeves, *Good God*, loc. 527.

Sanders added a further dimension to this understanding. Although following Jesus is often used to describe the walk of discipleship, he notes that through both our union with Christ at salvation and our ongoing abiding in him, Christians enter loving relationship with not just Jesus but the Father and the Spirit as well. He writes, "This is why, when we live as disciples of Christ, we can focus our attention on Jesus and in that very event encounter the Father and Spirit. This is why, if you follow Jesus, you follow him to his Father by the Spirit."[17] Together, these voices confirmed what had begun as a Spirit-led conviction: that discipleship—specifically the four goals I had formulated—emanate from abiding in the love of the triune God.

As these goals began to take shape, I conducted a survey of the precedent literature to compare my conclusions. This task affirmed that I was not only on track but potentially had something to contribute to this field. No work was found to show my definition unhelpful or erroneous; rather, much of it appeared to endorse the definition, either explicitly or implicitly. A diverse range of authors affirm the merit of the four goals of discipleship separately from one another, an overview that is beyond the scope of this book.

Several authors mention all four goals of discipleship implicitly in various writings, but without explicitly identifying them as goals of discipleship. Michael J. Wilkins, for example, writes,

> Discipleship consists of being molded by the apostolic teaching [embodying the image of God], being empowered by an experience with the living God [enjoying a relationship with God], and being a participant in a community of disciples [embracing the family of God]. On the other hand, it involves both a way to walk and a mission to fulfil [engaging the mission of God]. These definitions offer an approximation of what Jesus intended in his Great Commission."[18]

17. Sanders, "Follow the Trinity."
18. Wilkins, *Following the Master*, 519.

J. T. English provides another example of this, describing his view of discipleship as being in the context of the church (*embodying the family of God*), with the goal of mission (*engaging the mission of God*) and becoming like Christ (*embodying the image of God*), and empowered by the Holy Spirit (*enjoying a relationship with God*).[19]

Notably, three prominent voices on discipleship define its goals in ways that strongly echo the four I have developed. Putman and Harrington offer a similar definition, notably omitting any descriptor related to the goal of *embracing the family of God*. They write,

> We see that a disciple is a person who: (1) is following Christ (*head*); (2) is being changed by Christ (*heart*); and (3) is committed to the mission of Christ (*hands*). This is how we define a disciple. And this is what churches need to be seeking to make.[20]

This articulation, however, aligns closely with three of the four goals I have developed.

Steve Murrell presents another comparable definition in his book, *WikiChurch*. After reiterating the importance of defining discipleship—a point I have previously noted many authors stress—Murrell goes on to provide his definition with three descriptors of his own. He notes that for him and his church at Victory Manila, discipleship is a call to (1) follow Jesus, (2) fish for people, and (3) fellowship with others.[21] Interestingly, Murrell does not include the word "formed" in this alliterative definition or any phrase that represents the goal of *embodying the image of God*.

Most recently, John Mark Comer presents his definition of three goals of apprenticeship—the word he uses for discipleship—in his book *Practicing the Way*. He writes, "The meaning of discipleship is perfectly clear. . . . It's to organize your entire life around three driving goals: (1) Be with Jesus (2) Become like

---

19. English, *Deep Discipleship*, 51.

20. Putman and Harrington, *DiscipleShift*, 62–63; emphasis in original.

21. Murrell, *WikiChurch*, 60–64.

Him, and (3) Do as He did."[22] These goals closely correspond with those identified by Putman, Harrington, and myself, though again omitting explicit reference to community with fellow disciples as a distinct goal.

Putman and Harrington, Murrell, and Comer provide the most comprehensive and explicit definitions of the goals of discipleship in the precedent literature on the topic. They have contributed work that is crucial to the discussion on definitions of discipleship. They all, however, have excluded an element of the definition that another has included, and that I see as vital to a comprehensive definition.

The goals of discipleship are not a new to-do list, nor an updated set of commandments for the contemporary church. They are not linear steps to be followed in a clinical manner. Instead, they offer life-giving clarity—four distinct areas of the Christian life, shaped uniquely by the Holy Spirit in each believer's journey toward mature discipleship. As the church embraces these goals, it can move beyond the treadmill of inherited programs and methods, stepping into a more intentional and strategic approach to forming mature disciples for the glory of God.

22. Comer, *Practicing the Way*, 26.

9

The Pragmatic Task (2)

Four Environments of Discipleship

MY SECOND RESPONSE TO the question "How do I create a disciple-making church that equips individuals to self-initiate their Christian walk?" was to ascertain the environments required at Rhythm City Church to develop disciples who exemplify the four goals defined above. In considering the goals of discipleship and various sociocultural factors stemming from the COVID-19 pandemic, four environments of discipleship emerged that seemed salient for this era. These environments—(1) *Temple*, (2) *Table*, (3) *Technology*, and (4) *Training*—have been developed and refined over the last five years through an iterative reflection process.

Two observations led to *Table* becoming the first environment identified. Firstly, towards the end of a long lockdown period, I started to notice a recurring theme of lament among friends. Of the numerous areas of life that were now influenced by prohibitions or restrictions, there were not many that people sincerely missed. For example, it was uncommon to hear of someone yearning to return to the office for work. One craving, however, was prevalent: to have a meal with friends around a table. Secondly, a recurring theme among friends in youth ministry in Australia was that "family dinner" nights had replaced live music and games nights as the most well-attended gatherings in their youth ministries. One youth pastor reported that some of their teenagers had never eaten dinner around the table with their family. My sense that these phenomena highlighted part of God's heart for this era was reflected by Sweet, who prophetically declares, "The post-COVID church of the future will bring back the table."[1]

Several elements have emerged as central to the vision of Table at Rhythm City Church. Firstly, around the table is where *community is formed through meals*. When I was casting vision for this, the team responsible for outworking this discipleship environment was hesitant, suspecting the inclusion of a meal at every gathering would be overwhelming in our busy culture. After reading *A Meal with Jesus* by Tim Chester—a book that concreted my passion for this environment—they regathered and adamantly declared that meals cannot be omitted.[2] Gisela Kreglinger poetically describes the sacredness of meals, writing,

> In the Hebrew world that Jesus and his disciples inhabited, feasts and celebrations were important ways believers cultivated their spiritual lives. In them they remembered God's deeds of the past, embraced God's faithfulness in the present, and fostered expectant hope for God's redeeming intervention in the future.[3]

Secondly, around the table is where *identity is formed through stories*. "Table" is not simply a new name for the small-group system we used to call "connect groups," where we discuss questions based on weekend service sermons. On the contrary, it is a new environment attempting to draw out stories from people around the table, helping those present acquire what Sweet calls a "storied identity" as we participate in the narrative of God's people past and present.[4] Thirdly, around the table is where *ideas are formed*

1. Sweet, "Semiotic Exegesis," 5.
2. Chester, *Meal with Jesus*.
3. Kreglinger, *Spirituality of Wine*, 86.
4. Sweet, *Tablet to Table*, 49–50.

through conversation. Janet A. Flammang argues that rather than avoiding conversations around controversial topics like politics, the table—with its meals and storytelling—is the most suitable environment to learn how to share diverse ideas with civility.[5] Finally, around the table is where *Christ is formed through ministry.* Murrell contends that spiritual maturity takes place as disciples minister to others.[6] Rather than waiting for a separate time of prayer and worship after the meal, our vision is that people would learn how to minister to one another organically, as we eat around the table.

As the philosophy for Table started to take shape, I could not help but reflect on Acts 2:46, where the early church is reported to have met for meals in homes (Table) on top of their corporate worship in the temple. This sparked the idea of "Temple" being used as a designation for our weekend services, though with the nuance of gathering *as* the Temple (see Eph 2:21) rather than *in* the temple—a motif presented by Pieter Verster.[7] Along with the desire to eat with friends around the table, an equal hunger appeared to be rising for corporate worship. A Barna report that 81 percent of Christians placed a strong value on worshiping God alongside others confirmed my suspicions that Temple would remain a pivotal discipleship environment in the post-COVID era. Although the COVID-19 pandemic was revealing an overemphasis on weekend services, what was being highlighted was the need to adjust our services, not abandon them.

As I began to reimagine the shape of weekend services in the post-COVID era, several shifts emerged as opportunities for Rhythm City Church to more faithfully be the church. Firstly, I noticed the need to shift from *entertainment-focused services* to *exaltation-focused services.* The ideas underpinning this have been identified in the exploration of attractional church models above, with the consumerism of corporate influences having infiltrated our churches more than we might care to admit. An Instagram

5. Flammang, *Table Talk*, 1–6.

6. Murrell, *WikiChurch*, 132.

7. Verster, "Rebuilding the Community," 10.

post from the editor of Destiny Image, Larry Sparks, was a catalyst
for me in this train of thought. He comments on the singing element of our worship services, writing,

> "*How was worship?*" must be removed from our Chris-
> tian vernacular. "*How was worship?*" is a question only
> the object of our worship can answer. Our answer then to
> this question is revealing what was *really* worshiped. Our
> experience has become the gauge, thus revealing *that we
> in fact don't worship God, we worship our experience of
> worship.* In essence, we worship ourselves. Idolatry is a
> sneaky thing.[8]

This stirred a desire within me to build a community of disciples
who walk into a weekend service and immediately lift their voices
in worshipful song to God, regardless of the circumstances surrounding their personal lives, the quality of the audio-visual elements of the service, the song choice, or the level of goose bumps
or emotional ecstasy they experience. Gordon Dames notes that
the work of the church must be grounded in a "vigorous life of worship, prayer, proclamation and study of scripture and tradition."[9]
As Verster suggests, a shift from passively consuming an experience to actively participating in worship can be consequential for
our witness to the world in the post-COVID ecclesiological era.[10]

One practical way we are attempting to bring this shift at
Rhythm City Church is by removing the stage in our venues. This
may seem like a pedantic or insignificant change but is one I anticipate will usher in a significant paradigm shift for our church
members. Not only does the symbolism of a stage enhance the gap
between clergy and laity and exacerbate overly hierarchical models
of leadership and ministry, but it also subconsciously communi-
cates to church members that they are there to spectate rather than
participate. Stages—whether in ancient Greece or Renaissance
Italy—originated in the world of theatre, and "theatrical experience is based on the premise that the actors need a space in which

8. Sparks, "How was worship?"
9. Dames, "Quo Vadis," 86.
10. Verster, "Rebuilding the Community," 10.

to perform, and the audience must be in a position to see and hear them."[11] For a church the size of ours, it is plausible to create a more collaborative environment without a stage, promoting participation in every part of the worship service.

Secondly, I noticed the need to shift beyond *encouragement-focused services* towards *equipping-focused services*. Over the last few decades, encouragement has been a strength of church ministry, including weekend services. Congregants at Rhythm City Church, for example, have often walked out of services with an increased sense of faith, courage, and confidence to face life's challenges compared to when they arrived. The problem is that encouragement has often been derived from the ministry of church leaders rather than from "one another" (see Heb 10:25), enhancing the dependence on weekend services for an emotional lift. While receiving courage for Sunday is not a negative outcome, it is insufficient if not accompanied by receiving discipleship tools for Monday.

Intentionality around preaching and teaching is one practical way Rhythm City Church is trying to make this shift. One strategy we are using is to glean insights from the education sector to identify best practices for lecture-style education. Marianne M. Jennings, for instance, endorses the "sage on the stage" model of instruction that learner-centered theories have questioned in recent decades, noting the value of transferring knowledge from instructor to student.[12] Michael W. Kramer argues that the "sage on a stage" model only becomes ineffective when the trainer morphs into a "bore at the board."[13] This holds important keys for preaching at weekend services, as church leaders significantly enhance discipleship outcomes when they teach the Bible in ways that are conducive to effective learning. It is vital that these techniques are used to equip God's people to practice their faith through daily rhythms, not just to impress them with profound ideas on Sunday

11. Gillette and Dionne, *Theatrical Design and Production*, 51.

12. Jennings, "Sage on the Stage," 256.

13. Kramer, "Sage on the Stage," 246.

morning. And at Rhythm City Church, the sage—of course—is *off* the stage.

Another strategy we are exploring is rigorous sermon preparation to ensure practices for applying biblical insights are a major element of every message. To move beyond encouragement and into equipping, biblical revelation must be partnered with practical application, ensuring that church members have clear discipleship tools for use upon leaving the weekend gathering. Answers to the question "How do I live differently based on what you are proposing?" must be easily identifiable to listeners.

A final example of our attempt to reshape weekend services is a shift *away from evangelism-focused services towards empowerment-focused services.* We have declared the end of "invite-and-bring" as the primary evangelism strategy of our church, where members must bring non-Christian friends to a weekend service for professionals to lead them to salvation. One major contributing factor to this was answering the question "Who is the weekend service primarily for?" in the same way Wilson does: it is primarily for Christians.[14] Considering that, rather than reducing our evangelism to two hours per week in the church building, it followed logically that it would be more fruitful to use those two hours to empower Christians with tools to live missionally throughout the remainder of the week.[15] This is not to say that non-Christians are not welcome at weekend services. As Wilson notes, "The worship service must be conducted with the unbeliever in mind, but it doesn't need to be conducted with the unbeliever in focus."[16] Non-Christians will hopefully encounter the presence of God, exhibited through the worship, love, and unity of God's people rather than attractional methods.

During the COVID-19 lockdowns—while the ideas of Temple and Table were swirling around in my mind—a drive home from a welcomed outing to the supermarket became an unexpected moment of clarity. It was during this ordinary drive

14. Wilson, *Gospel-Driven Church*, 91.

15. Stiles, *Evangelism*, 42.

16. Wilson, *Prodigal Church*, 55.

that a third discipleship environment came into focus: *Technology*. At the time, I found myself slightly uneasy about emerging ideas that seemed to frame technology as the singular lesson God was teaching the Church through the pandemic. While I appreciated the creative adaptations churches were making, I feared we were at risk of reducing a deep, disruptive, and formational season to a conversation about live streaming platforms. Pillay captures this concern well, warning, "If all the church has learnt during this time of COVID-19 is how to live-stream sermons, worship songs, religious rites and requests for tithes, we have lost the Kairos moment."[17] Still, I sensed that although it was not the *only* lesson God was bringing to the Church through the pandemic, the benefits of using technology for ecclesiological outcomes were among the insights being highlighted.

As new technologies played a prominent role in the church's response to the COVID-19 pandemic, digital expressions were gaining respect as valid and important tools for the post-COVID era. Anthony Le Duc captures this development, noting that technologies once seen merely as accessories were now considered necessities for sustaining and building ecclesial life.[18] Just as the printing press propelled the Protestant Reformation five hundred years earlier, new technologies were emerging as crucial instruments for igniting a new reformation in the Church.[19]

Three elements of the Technology discipleship environment settled over time as I considered the Rhythm City Church digital strategy. Firstly, Technology is how *the church is enabled to gather despite physical limitations through hybrid models*. John Dyer defines a hybrid church as "a local church that includes both digital and in-person experiences."[20] The Barna Group are calling this dual approach of physical and digital "phygital."[21] From the moment in-person gatherings resumed after lockdowns, every

---

17. Pillay, "Church More Flexible," 274.
18. Le Duc, "Church's Online Presence," 17.
19. Zandroto, "COVID-19," 350.
20. Dyer, "Exploring Mediated Ekklesia," 13.
21. Barna Group, *Six Questions*, 4.

Rhythm City Church location implemented a hybrid approach for various church gatherings, including weekend services, leadership meetings, and prayer meetings. This element does not involve broadcasting in-person services around the world but fostering connections within our church family. In a relatively short time, it has helped overcome the geographical limitations of our global multi-site model, assisted church members who are unwell or traveling to remain connected in church life, and enabled one of our locations to gather amid venue availability issues.

Secondly, Technology is how *other discipleship environments are enhanced using existing and emerging technologies.* Technology cannot be completely separated from Temple, Table, or Training. The hybrid model above, for example, plays a supportive role within Temple. Church members who travel often take part in a virtual Table, eating meals and engaging in conversation through video conferencing platforms. A significant part of our explorations in Training to date has involved online training resources, a growing educational trend.[22] When one location was restricted from utilizing its weekend service venue for six weeks, the church met around tables, with each table connecting through Technology. It could be said that Technology turned Table into Temple.

Finally, Technology is how *non-Christians are engaged through digital content that demystifies God and the Church.* The missional possibilities that come with technological innovation are among the strongest themes coming through post-COVID literature on digital ecclesiology. Rainer—although supportive of hybrid models—suggests that the digital components must move beyond continuing existing ministries and into new missional frontiers.[23] Sweet agrees, arguing that mirroring weekend services will not be sufficient for this new era and that technology must be used in missional ways to reach those outside the existing church community.[24]

---

22. Boca, "Factors Influencing Students' Behavior," 3.

23. Rainer, *Post-Quarantine Church*, 27.

24. Sweet, "Semiotic Exegesis," 5.

This idea is currently in a conceptual stage at Rhythm City Church and will require serious consideration and collaboration for it to take shape over the coming years. Utilizing YouTube and social media however—or whatever technologies rise to prominence next—lies at the heart of this element. Dave Adamson—one of the first online pastors in the world—argues that "YouTube is the most important platform for any church leader wanting to use digital tools to make disciples."[25] Adamson was the keynote speaker at a conference I attended, and I approached him with concerns I had about whether a church the size of ours could make a digital impact in these spaces. The insights he shared—some of which are detailed in his book *Metachurch*—built confidence in me that Rhythm City Church could indeed use technology to engage missionally with people who feel far from God and church.

As Rhythm City Church continues to develop this discipleship environment, we will need to pay attention to Buhle Mpofu's important caution concerning digital approaches. He helpfully points out that the costs required to obtain devices and internet access to utilize technology are economically restrictive for the poor, potentially leading to their exclusion from these spaces.[26] With a heart for the global church, this is an important consideration for us moving forward.

For several months, we began discussions as a leadership group at Rhythm City Church to discuss these three environments of discipleship: Temple, Table, and Technology. Although no additions were obvious, something about the model seemed incomplete. One day it dawned on me that there was no context for the explicit and primary focus of Christian education. Having twenty years of combined experience in primary school teaching and adult education, the omission seemed ironic. In response, *Training* was added as a fourth and final discipleship environment.

Training is another emerging area within Rhythm City Church, with two largely unapplied elements currently being imagined among our leadership teams. Firstly, we see Training as

25. Adamson, *Metachurch*, 87.
26. Mpofu, "Mission on the Margins," 3.

being where *disciples progress in spiritual maturity through digital and in-person courses and seminars.* The connection between education and discipleship has been affirmed by an array of scholars over the past decade. For example, Andrew Burggraff asserts that developing a discipleship curriculum is essential to fulfilling the Great Commission in the twenty-first century.[27] Norsworthy, Dowden, and Luetz also emphasize the crucial role of education in discipleship. They note that in historical eras when pedagogies were based on holistic anthropologies, universities "invited people into a way of life to make them lovers of God who desired to learn so that they could be image bearers of God to and for the world around them."[28] These outcomes directly correlate to Rhythm City Church's discipleship goals of enjoying a relationship with God, embodying the image of God, and engaging the mission of God. Leonard Sweet stresses the universal importance of implementing education for discipleship within the church in the post-COVID era, writing,

> Every church is now a seminary ("seminary" literally means "seed-bed" for faith), and every pastor a dean, yoking a common core of theological content for the 21st century to both customised mentoring and cohort-based, peer-to-peer (P2P) learning based on the world as both church and our classroom.[29]

Not only do we envision Training as being key for making disciples, but we also see it as indispensable for developing leaders who will be responsible for facilitating discipleship in the church. Therefore, Training is also where *leaders produce knowledge, skills, and character through courses, intensives, and mentorships.* Ray Easley notes the urgency of leadership training in the majority world, highlighting a major reason as the growth of Christianity.[30] With God's purposes accelerating through the COVID-19 pandemic,

27. Burggraff, "Developing Discipleship Curriculum," 397.
28. Norsworthy et al., "Learning and Loves," 5.
29. Sweet, "Semiotic Exegesis," 10.
30. Easley, "Theological Education," 23.

churches around the world could be justified in expecting similar trends. Keith Krispin Jr cautions, however, that "despite the importance of Christian leadership development, programs and plans for developing leaders sometimes seem unclear, unfocused, or random."[31] This validates the slow approach being implemented by our team, a result of our desire to implement well-considered programs.

These four environments—Temple, Table, Technology, and Training—form a rhythm that shapes the church's programmatic life and key connection points. Each one is distinct, creating the context for their own unique discipleship outcomes, while also complementing the others to support the overall task of forming disciples. They are not the only environments that may emerge in a church community, but they offer a meaningful starting point for this era. Rather than a rigid, one-size-fits-all model, they serve as a flexible framework—providing helpful categories and outcomes that churches can interpret and implement according to their own context. As such, they should be held with humility and openness, always subject to the leading of the Spirit and the needs of the people they are meant to serve.

31. Krispin, "Christian Leader Development," 19.

Conclusion

ARUNDHATI ROY WRITES EVOCATIVELY in summarizing the
COVID-19 pandemic's impact on humanity:

> Historically, pandemics have forced humans to break
> with the past and imagine their world anew. This one is
> no different. It is a portal, a gateway between one world
> and the next. We can choose to walk through it, drag-
> ging the carcasses of our prejudice and hatred, our ava-
> rice, our data banks and dead ideas, our dead rivers and
> smoky skies behind us. Or we can walk through lightly,
> with little luggage, ready to imagine another world. And
> ready to fight for it.[1]

Nowhere are Roy's words more relevant than in the church—an
understanding this book has sought to awaken. The COVID-19
pandemic was not merely a health crisis but a bridge between two
epochs of church history. Church leaders must resist the temptation to retreat across that bridge and instead remain committed to
discovering new ecclesiological paradigms for this post-COVID era.

Jason A. Miller and Judy L. Glanz report a concern among
church leaders who initially recognized the reformational nature
of the COVID-19 pandemic of "losing the new growths—both
personal and spiritual—to a return of business as usual."[2] Several

---

1. Roy, "Pandemic Is a Portal."
2. Miller and Glanz, "Personal Experiences," 508.

years after the discontinuation of the COVID-19 pandemic's global health emergency status, the temptation to view the COVID-19 era as a resolved inconvenience is evident. Church leaders must refuse to do so at all costs lest they wallow in dated church practices until the next wake-up call. A life-long commitment to reformational thinking is the only antidote. As Leonard Sweet notes, "The only way to prepare for a future of constant 'the end of the world as we know it?' moments is by developing a high Contextual Quotient (CQ), and deepening our Contextual Intelligence (CI) so we can choose 'the next right thing' in a world of volcanic volatility."[3]

The story you have just read offers my interpretation of the COVID-19 moment thus far—both the conclusions I arrived at while leading Rhythm City Church through the pandemic and the journey that led me there. I am convinced that discipleship is one of the foremost revelations on God's heart in this era and that the COVID-19 pandemic offered a rare and valuable opportunity to embed reformational DNA within the church. But a discipleship-centered reformation will come at a cost. Church leaders seeking to establish churches shaped by the ideas presented in this work will encounter at least four common considerations as they move forward.

To begin with, this pathway will demand that both leaders and congregations confront the discipleship crisis our past models have produced—and take responsibility for their complicity in it. Reformation will emerge only through repentance, even of our most well-intended yet misdirected efforts. The shortcomings of past models cannot be justified, or the temptation to carry them into the new will prove too strong. Instead, we must earnestly seek God for wisdom and discernment to understand what can be carried forward and what must be repented of and jettisoned for the journey ahead.

Next, a church deeply committed to discipleship must hold the conviction that discipleship is the God-given mission for every church in every age. While that may seem self-evident, it bears emphasizing. Reductionist views of discipleship—such as

3. Sweet, "Semiotic Exegesis," 1.

equating it solely with spiritual formation—will not carry us into the new era. Discipleship is not the only theme in Christian theology and practice, but it is the church's primary assignment: the task through which the church is built, and the kingdom of God is expanded.

In addition, effective disciple-making practices begin with the hard work of defining what discipleship is. I argue that this process should start with the goals of discipleship, and I offer my own attempt at this task for the reader's consideration. This definitional work, however, must extend to every aspect of the disciple-making task. Jim Putman and Bobby Harrington highlight the importance of this clarity:

> Anytime you gather a group of people to accomplish a goal, you first need to get everyone on the same page. You need to define what you want to accomplish and how you are going to do it. Whenever any group sets out to work together to accomplish a goal, the tasks, methods, and objectives need to be defined, clearly communicated, and understood by everyone involved.[4]

As we arrive at rich and robust definitions of discipleship, we position ourselves to move forward with clarity and intentionality—rather than depending on chance to hit the target.

Finally, church leaders and congregations participating in a discipleship reformation must commit to the vision with long-term resolve. This is not the launch of a new program but a reorientation of how we *are* the church—a way of being that embraces ongoing rhythms of reformation. Cultivating a culture of risk is essential, allowing the necessary innovation and experimentation to emerge. We will need the courage to boldly implement new initiatives and, at times, to close others decisively. Yet in all of this, our methods must be held loosely—always submitted to the priority of making mature disciples of Jesus. May the commission given by Jesus continually breathe life and energy into our task:

4. Putman and Harrington, *DiscipleShift*, 49.

I have been given all authority in heaven and on earth. Therefore, go and make disciples of all the nations, baptizing them in the name of the Father and the Son and the Holy Spirit. Teach these new disciples to obey all the commands I have given you. And be sure of this: I am with you always, even to the end of the age. (Matt 28:18–20)

Appendix 1
Discipleship and Formation

And when he found him, he brought him to Antioch. So for a whole year Barnabas and Saul met with the church and taught great numbers of people. The disciples were called Christians first at Antioch.

ACTS 11:26 (NIV)

THE RENEWED EMPHASIS ON discipleship in the post-COVID landscape is encouraging, yet one of the central concerns of this book—the need for clarity and consensus around how we define discipleship—remains a pressing priority for the church. This clarity must be pursued not only through our explicit definitions but also in the implicit comparisons we draw between discipleship and other concepts. One such comparison is the common tendency—both in academic writing and popular church discourse—to equate *discipleship* with *formation*. At first glance, the issue may seem minor, but a deeper exploration raises significant definitional concerns. Although this distinction was addressed earlier in the book, the ongoing confusion in many church contexts makes it necessary to examine it more closely.

An important starting point is to note that the term *disciple* is synonymous with the term *Christian*. In verb form, the Greek word for *disciple* means "to learn"; in noun form, it can refer to a student who learns from a teacher.[1] With that in mind, a disciple is not a different kind of Christian, nor is it a specific category or subtype within Christianity. Rather, both words describe the same kind of person—someone who follows the person and teaching of Jesus Christ. As demonstrated in the Scripture above, the early church used both terms to identify those who embraced what is now known as Christianity. A Christian is a disciple, and a disciple is a Christian. Whether one refers to a person as a Christian, a disciple, a follower of Jesus, a believer, someone who has been born again, or someone who has received salvation, each expression points to the same reality: a person who belongs to Christ.

Discipleship, by extension, can be understood as the experience of being a disciple and making disciples—from the point of conversion to the end of life. It encompasses the full scope of what the Christian life is meant to involve. This illuminates my assertion that *discipleship* is *not* the same as what is commonly referred to as *formation*—or with its related concepts such as *spiritual formation, sanctification, transformation, bearing fruit, maturity,* or *spiritual growth.* These terms, although not entirely interchangeable in themselves, relate more to the image of Christ being increasingly formed and expressed in us. Whether the emphasis is on the process or its outcome, they all point to the development of attitudes and behaviors that reflect the character of Jesus. In this way, these terms represent a vital aspect of the Christian journey—one that deeply influences many other areas of faith. Nevertheless, terms like *formation* describe part of what occurs within the life of a Christian, whereas *disciple* refers to the overall identity of the person being formed and *discipleship* to the entire Christian journey. The two are connected, but they are not the same.

To illustrate this point further, consider the following examples. As noted in the chapter on *Disciple-Making Churches*, one author observes, "Not to mention, it seems that discipleship (formation) seems to be of minimal importance in many churches

---

1. Russ, *Discipleship Defined*, loc. 186.

when compared to evangelism and church growth strategies."[2] While the idea of this statement is important, the parenthetical use of *formation* suggests that it is synonymous with *discipleship*. This conflation is further illustrated by a well-known church leader who recently began an Instagram reel by explicitly noting his belief that there is a difference between salvation and discipleship. He proceeded to explain that salvation involves receiving the benefits of Jesus' death and resurrection, whereas discipleship involves the self-denying lifestyle of the believer taking up their own cross. In this framing, not only is discipleship equated with formation, but it is also inevitably distinguished from salvation, implying that salvation can occur without discipleship.

Herein lies the problem: when we suggest that there are *Christians who are saved* and *disciples who are formed*, we inadvertently create an opt-out clause when it comes to formation. If there is a version of faith on offer with all the benefits and less cost, consumer Christianity has shown that many will gladly take it. Who would not take the "cheap seats" if they had all the perks of the full-priced ones? This separation suggests a two-tiered system: entry-level Christianity for the masses—with forgiveness and assurance—and then a higher, more committed version called discipleship, reserved for those who want to be "serious" Christians or pursue leadership. At best, this division keeps people in a prolonged state of spiritual immaturity. At worst, it leads them into a version of religion that is altogether different from Christianity. That may sound confronting—but perhaps it is the kind of disruption we need if we are going to give proper attention to the language of discipleship.

The tendency to use *discipleship* and *formation* interchangeably often stems from a sincere desire to see followers of Jesus grow and bear fruit, particularly among those who are not yet doing so. To be sure, *it is* important to distinguish between those who are actively growing in the four goals of discipleship and those who have, whether knowingly or not, settled for something far less—particularly in a time when consumer Christianity is so prevalent. While

2. Davis, *Trinitarian Formation*, xix.

it may seem pedantic, however, the previous examples highlight the importance of the language we use to do so.

Building on the Instagram reel example above, a more effective way to emphasize the importance of self-denial and bearing fruit might be to distinguish between terms like *forgiveness* and *formation*. These terms, or others like them, highlight two distinct but related aspects of discipleship—included in what I have described as the goals of discipleship: *enjoying a relationship with God* and *embodying the image of God*, respectively. There are certainly seasons in life when the benefits of salvation—what Jesus accomplished on the cross—and the fruit of salvation—our response in taking up our own cross—seem out of alignment. The concept of a "deathbed salvation"—such as the thief on the cross who received the promise of paradise with no opportunity to demonstrate transformed living—is a clear example. At other times, we may withhold parts of our lives from God's transforming work for a season. Sadly, there are also moments when the heart hardens or strays, leading us temporarily off course.

While we remain alive on this earth, addressing a discipleship deficit through the lens of the four goals in this book allows us to hold grace and truth together. It gives space for compassion toward each person's process without dismissing the biblical call to bear fruit and live like Jesus. Peter makes this connection between forgiveness and formation explicit. After listing qualities that should be growing in a disciple's life, he writes, "The more you grow like this, the more productive and useful you will be in your knowledge of our Lord Jesus Christ. But those who fail to develop in this way are shortsighted or blind, forgetting that they have been cleansed from their old sins" (2 Pet 1:8–9). *Forgetting.* There is no condemnation in that word—but neither is there permission to ignore what matters. Those who have been forgiven must remember what Christ has done—and live out of that revelation. Despite temporary interruptions to the progress, that is what all disciples (Christians) are called to do, and there is no alternative option. There is, however, plenty of grace for the journey.

Appendix 2
Reformation and Revival

But forget all that—
it is nothing compared to what I am going to do
For I am about to do something new.
See, I have already begun! Do you not see it?
I will make a pathway through the wilderness.
I will create rivers in the dry wasteland.

ISA 43 18–19

WHILE THIS PASSAGE IN Isaiah originally speaks to Judah's impending return from exile in Babylon, it also offers valuable insight into the ways God has moved throughout the history of his people. The COVID-19 pandemic stands as a contemporary example of such divine movement—ushering in not only a "new normal" for human civilization but also signaling a fresh era in the outworking of God's purposes for the Church. Yet these shifts are often not entirely novel or unheard of; rather, they are significant truths or practices that have faded from focus among God's people. Len Sweet calls them "old-new," while Jacques Beukes refers to them as the "forgotten old."[1] In the ways of God, "new" often refers to a refreshing of, and returning to, ancient ideas that have come to be neglected.

1. Sweet, "Semiotic Exegesis," 8; Beukes, "To Be," 1.

Throughout the Scriptures, a recurring pattern emerges in the way God brings about something new: first, God *forms*, and then God *fills*. In Gen 2:7, God forms Adam from the dust and then breathes life into him. A similar pattern is seen in 2 Chr 5 where Solomon finishes building the temple and only then does the ark enter, and God's presence fills the space. In Ezek 37:1–14, the bones are assembled but remain zombie-like until God breathes life into them. Likewise, in the New Testament, the Church is birthed on the day of Pentecost when believers are gathered in one place, and only then does the Holy Spirit fill the house where they are meeting.

This rhythm of forming and filling highlights the vital roles of both reformation and revival as two inseparable aspects of God's restorative work in the church, particularly in this post-COVID era. Ellen G. White, cofounder of the Seventh-day Adventist Church, articulates the distinction and connection between the two:

> A revival and a reformation must take place, under the ministration of the Holy Spirit. Revival and reformation are two different things. Revival signifies a renewal of spiritual life, a quickening of the powers of mind and heart, a resurrection from spiritual death. Reformation signifies a reorganization, a change in ideas and theories, habits, and practices. Reformation will not bring forth the good fruit of righteousness unless it is connected with the revival of the Spirit. Revival and reformation are to do their appointed work, and in doing this work they must blend.[2]

P. J. Buys affirms the necessity of both, observing that reformation without revival can result in shallow, external change that lacks genuine spiritual passion, while revival without reformation may produce emotional enthusiasm without a sustained, transformative walk with God.[3] This insight became clear to me two years after the COVID-19 pandemic began, as I realized we at Rhythm City Church were at risk of engaging in a powerless and lifeless

2. White, *Selected Messages*, 128.
3. Buys, "Reformation and Revival," 188.

reprogramming of the church if it was not accompanied by a renewed fervor for God.

Another helpful way to distinguish between reformation and revival is by viewing them through the lens of Scripture's two great mandates. As I have engaged more deeply with this topic, I have come to see reformation as connected to the Great Commission—to make disciples of all nations (Matt 28:18–20)—while revival reflects the great commandment: to love God and love others as ourselves (Matt 22:37–40). Reformation involves the Church refocusing on its mission of discipleship, aligning both theology and practice with the truth of Scripture. Revival, on the other hand, is the work of the Holy Spirit igniting fresh love for the Father and the Son within the hearts of believers, providing the energy and impetus needed for that mission.

A final and important consideration in comparing reformation and revival is the question of order: Which one comes first, and does it matter? I have heard many church leaders advocate for the priority of revival, and in some ways, God's sovereignty allows for either one to precede the other. The form-and-fill pattern explored above, however, leads me to believe that the ideal order is reformation preceding revival. While it might seem logical that a spiritual awakening of the heart would catalyze broader reform in the Church, this has not been my observation in seasons of spiritual renewal. More on my personal experience shortly, but in many cases, revival does not lead to lasting reformation. Instead, it often produces a kind of spiritual hangover. Just as weekend services have, in recent decades, become a crutch for spiritual infants and the spiritually unwell, so too have revival moments become a spiritual crutch in past seasons. When the manifest "move of God" seems to lift, many are left confused and discouraged, unsure of how to move forward in strength and purpose once the spiritual and emotional high is gone. As we engage in reformation—putting discipleship at the forefront of church practice—revival can breathe life into what has been formed, enhancing the work without depending on heightened spiritual experiences to carry out the mission entrusted to us. After all, Jesus is with us—always, even to the very end of the age (Matt 28:20).

What does revival look like in the post-COVID era? Revival is a loaded word for many Christians. Some cherish the idea, finding purpose and identity in revivalism. Others reject it—sometimes vehemently—because of unhealthy expressions they have encountered. I can sympathize with both perspectives, being born-again into a church experiencing revival in the late 1990s. It was marked by characteristics stereotypical of revival culture: long meetings, signs, wonders and miracles, souls saved *en masse*, intense repentance from sin, extreme demonstrations of holiness like burning non-Christian music, and radical exploits of prayer and fasting. On the one hand, I am deeply grateful for those roots, which instilled in me a lasting value for Spirit-filled life and ministry. At the same time, that environment introduced me to a culture outside of that congregation where unhealthy expressions were often woven throughout the good. Still, amid the good, the bad, and the ugly, I yearn for seasons where the church is drawn into an increased awareness of the presence and work of the Holy Spirit.

Another type of revival, however, strikes me as even more important for the times we live in. I have come to call it a *perpetual, personal revival*. One of the most captivating natural wonders I have encountered is the Nile River. As the longest river in the world, it flows through eleven countries—from East Africa in the south to the Mediterranean Sea in the north. For thousands of years, it has carried immense religious, economic, historical, cultural, and geopolitical significance. Its source—particularly of the branch known as the White Nile—has been a subject of fascination and debate since antiquity. I have visited the site on Lake Victoria—at Jinja, Uganda—identified by explorer John Speke in the mid-1800s as the source of the White Nile. A short boat ride takes you to a spot where bubbles rise to the surface, revealing underground springs feeding the lake. Yet over time, the notion of a single source has proven too simple. Other landmarks have emerged with equal—or even stronger—claims. Among them are the Rwenzori Mountains, also known as the Mountains of the Moon, which straddle the border between Uganda and the Democratic Republic of the Congo. Their contribution to the White Nile is different: rather than underground springs, they offer rainfall from the heavens, cascading down the slopes into rivers that eventually join the Nile's flow.

When many people hear the word *revival*, they tend to picture something like the Rwenzori Mountains—an external outpouring from the heavens touching the earth. These are powerful seasons of divine encounter that contribute richly to the flow of God's river, and we should welcome them with joy. Yet I carry a conviction that, in this hour, there is a new kind of revival the church must prioritize. It resembles Lake Victoria more than the Rwenzoris—an outflowing rather than an outpouring. It is the bubbling up of the Holy Spirit within the life of every believer, regardless of the broader spiritual climate of the church. This kind of revival appears to be the ongoing invitation of the New Testament era—something always available, to anyone, at any time. As Jesus declared,

> On the last day, the climax of the festival, Jesus stood and shouted to the crowds, "Anyone who is thirsty may come to me! Anyone who believes in me may come and drink! For the Scriptures declare, 'Rivers of living water will flow from his heart.'" (When he said "living water," he was speaking of the Spirit, who would be given to everyone believing in him. But the Spirit had not yet been given, because Jesus had not yet entered into his glory.) (John 7:38–39)

This passage suggests that God may be more interested in getting his Spirit out of us than down to us.

Imagine a church that does not require an external revival—because it is already awake. So often, we hear about the need for a move of God, but perhaps the true need is for a move of the Church. What if everything necessary to live with passion, fervency, and revival has already been given—and already resides within us? It is entirely possible to love God with all our heart, soul, and mind—and to love our neighbor as ourselves—regardless of our circumstances or the prevailing spiritual climate.

Appendix 3

Reformation and a Pioneering Spirit

A time to kill and a time to heal.
A time to tear down and a time to build up.

Eccl 3:3

AFTER SEVENTY YEARS IN exile in Babylon, the people of Judah were finally given the opportunity to return to Jerusalem and rebuild the temple—just as the prophet Jeremiah had foretold (see Jer 25:1–14). God used King Cyrus of Persia as his chosen instrument to make this possible. Having conquered Babylon and brought an end to its empire, the Persians opened the door for Judah's restoration. We read the account of the edict being given by King Cyrus in Ezra 1:3, which records it as follows: "Any of you who are his people may go to Jerusalem in Judah to rebuild this Temple of the Lord, the God of Israel, who lives in Jerusalem. And may your God be with you!" The initial return was led by Zerubbabel (Ezra 1–6), followed by a second and third wave under the leadership of Ezra (Ezra 7–10) and Nehemiah (Neh 1–7), respectively.[1]

The narrative of the first return phase—to rebuild the temple in ruins—offers profound insight for navigating the post-COVID reformation of the church. Reformation involves both tearing

1. Kitchen, *Reliability*, 71.

68

down and building up. It begins with acknowledging, repenting of, and dismantling beliefs and practices that have drifted from truth. But it also requires faith, creativity, and a willingness to step into new ways led by the Spirit. A rhythm of reformation makes this process a holy habit. It is not for the fainthearted; reformers must carry a pioneering spirit. The remnant who returned from Babylon embodied such a spirit. Everything they knew had been torn down by the Babylonians, yet God entrusted them with the task of rebuilding. In the same way, the COVID-19 pandemic stripped away much from the contemporary church. Now, a new remnant is being called to rebuild. Importantly, this rhythm of reformation is not limited to crisis seasons of captivity or pandemic—it is a cyclical pattern that can be engaged even in times of peace and stability. The story of the exilic return offers timely and timeless insight into the pioneering spirit required for reformational tearing down and building up—a pattern that echoes throughout history and into our present moment.

Firstly, we see in this story that a *pioneering spirit requires letting go of comfort*. One might imagine that the edict of King Cyrus sparked widespread excitement and a mass return to Jerusalem. After all, this was the long-awaited moment—a chance to go back home and rebuild the temple, one of the most central and sacred elements of Jewish life. Surely, everyone would be inspired to seize the opportunity and take part in this historic task. Surprisingly, that was not the reality. According to Ezra 2:64–65, only about fifty thousand people volunteered to be part of the return and rebuilding project. While estimates vary, most scholars agree that this represented only a small fraction of the total Judean population living in Babylon at the time. As Charles Fensham observes, "Only a small group returned, and many pious and prosperous Jews remained in Babylon and vicinity."[2] Elelwani Farisani observes that while Babylon was far from a paradise, exile did not equate to slavery. The Judeans experienced a surprising degree of comfort and stability—securing employment and agricultural opportunities, building homes, and raising families within a foreign

2. Fensham, *Ezra and Nehemiah*, 45.

empire.[3] When one weighs the familiarity and security of life in Babylon against the uncertainty, hardship, and danger of returning to a ruined homeland, it becomes clear why so many chose to stay behind.[4] It is one thing to respond to change when it is imposed—such as during the COVID-19 pandemic or the era of exile; it is another altogether to initiate change from inner conviction, even when circumstances do not demand it—such as in the post-COVID or return eras.

This story reminds us that the human longing for comfort is nothing new. Yet, throughout my lifetime, there has been an increasing gravitational pull toward comfort—particularly evident in Western culture. This trend is undoubtedly shaped by a range of factors, including relative geopolitical stability, a growing emphasis on individualism, and the pervasive rise of consumer capitalism.[5] Certainly, Scripture tells us that God is the "source of all comfort" (2 Cor 1:3). Importantly, however, the comfort God offers is not the removal of difficulty but the strengthening of our souls in the face of it.[6] In contrast, the kind of comfort widely pursued in contemporary culture is defined by the absence of struggle, inconvenience, or pain.[7] Not only does this comfort afford a certain amount of damage to our souls, it distorts the biblical narrative that presents trials, suffering, and hardship not as detours but as essential to the human—and Christian—journey. As Brett McCracken observes, there are discipleship outcomes born out of crisis that cannot be produced from comfort:

> Why is it important that we avoid falling into comfortable Christianity? Because comfortable Christianity is far from the costly, inconvenient, idol-crushing, cross-shaped path for disciples of Jesus. Comfortable Christianity has little prophetic to say to a comfortable,

3. Farisani, "Sociological Analysis," 382–84.

4. Friedman and Hersovitz, "Rebuilding of the Temple," 6.

5. To examine the link between comfort and consumer Christianity, see McCracken, *Uncomfortable*.

6. Berding, "Comfort."

7. Boni, "Era of Comfort," 50.

consumerist world. Comfortable Christianity has little
urgency in mission and little aptitude for growth.[8]

It may be said that God desires us to be comforted, but not necessarily comfortable.

It is important to recognize that the lure of the event-driven,
attractional model of church will remain strong for years to come.
This model is familiar, and with familiarity comes comfort. Like
the Israelites who, after leaving Egypt, preferred the predictabil-
ity of slavery to the uncertainty of the wilderness, we too can be
drawn back to what feels safe rather than step forward into the
unknown territory of a discipleship-centered church. This temptation is vividly captured in the imagery of two generations returning from exile, each responding differently to the laying of the
second temple's foundation:

> But many of the older priests, Levites, and other lead-
> ers who had seen the first Temple wept aloud when they
> saw the new Temple's foundation. The others, however,
> were shouting for joy. The joyful shouting and weeping
> mingled together in a loud noise that could be heard far
> in the distance." (Ezra 3:12-13)

Those who had seen the old longed for its return, even though the
new carried God's promise for the future. In much the same way,
many will mourn the loss of the familiar models of church, even
as God invites us into a new expression shaped by discipleship. In
this new era, only by embracing discomfort will a generation of
pioneers rise—leaders who reject the ease of consumer Christianity and embody the courageous, countercultural way of Jesus.

Secondly, the exilic return narrative reveals that *a pioneering
spirit is essential not only for church leaders but for every member
of the church community* Ezra 2 provides a record of those who
returned from exile to Jerusalem, and verse 2—when considered
alongside Neh 7:7—identifies twelve leaders who oversaw the return. Most notable among them is Zerubbabel, governor of Judah
and chief leader. Without leadership that possesses both the vision

8. McCracken, "8 Signs."

to perceive a reformational assignment and the courage to call others toward it, no community will rebuild by accident. Leadership is essential for reformational change.

While the centrality of leadership may be obvious, an equally important—yet often more hidden—truth is the need for the entire community to embody the same pioneering spirit. Though they may not be the source of the vision, it is essential that a pioneering people embrace the Spirit-birthed vision carried by pioneering leaders. This is not merely about rallying around a strategic plan but about responding to a divine revelation of what God is calling the community into. This dynamic is evident among those identified in the remainder of Ezra 2—the people—who left what was familiar, gave sacrificially, and aligned themselves with the vision of rebuilding the temple. Their response came at personal cost rather than personal gain, and this willingness appears to be a crucial factor in the ultimate success of the mission.

A pioneering people must be led by the Spirit, willing to abandon comfort when it conflicts with their kingdom assignment, and inclined to trust and support godly leaders seeking to be faithful and obedient to God's leading. When leaders attempt to bring people into reformational assignments without a shared vision, collective willingness, and mutual trust, the relational and missional outcomes can be deeply damaging—sometimes even catastrophic. The exodus provides a clear example of this dynamic. Moses was called by God to secure the freedom of the Israelites from Egypt—a pioneering task not unlike Zerubbabel's leadership in Babylon. Unfortunately, only Joshua and Caleb were described as having a "different spirit" (see Num 14:24), while most of the people were marked by unbelief (see Heb 3:19). Whatever the precise nature of this different spirit, it clearly included a pioneering component. Most of the Israelites were not responsive to God's leading, preferred comfort over calling, and harbored a posture of mistrust toward Moses. The result was twofold: (1) a continual relational strain marked by conflict and complaint and (2) ultimate missional failure for that generation—rectified only by the one that followed. In this post-COVID era, it is essential that the church consists of both leaders and congregation members who carry a pioneering spirit for the reformational task at hand.

One final thought on this point: it strikes me that the exiles who left Babylon brought their families with them. As obvious as that may seem, it holds significant relevance for the times we are living in. Many who pioneered the contemporary church in the late twentieth century did so at personal cost to their families. There was a prevailing mindset of giving everything for the cause of building the church. In time, it became evident that some of these marital and parental sacrifices were unnecessary. As a result, my generation of emerging church leaders was rightly taught not to *sacrifice family on the altar of ministry*—a valuable lesson passed down by those who learned it through painful, firsthand experience. It now seems, however, that our generation is in danger of falling into the opposite ditch: *sacrificing ministry on the altar of family*. A pioneering spirit is being dampened by valid, yet extreme, concerns that our children cannot handle the cost of a pioneering journey. The people of Judah seemed to understand that God calls families. While there is wisdom in discerning how to follow God with children, we must also trust that the One who calls parents knows both the mission ahead and the children they are called to steward. I cannot help but believe there is a divine compatibility between the two. Every generation needs new pioneers, and our children will catch the pioneering spirit not merely in classrooms, but by witnessing the lives and ministries of pioneering parents, whether in formal church leadership or not.

Thirdly, the account of the return from exile reveals that *a pioneering spirit requires oneness*. Ezra 3:1 is a potent description of the culture within the community as the temple rebuilding began: "When the seventh month came and the Israelites were in their towns, the people gathered together as one in Jerusalem." *As one.* Several other New Testament passages describe the importance God places on oneness being present among his people, a word that reflects his heart even more deeply than *unity*. The apostle Paul urges believers in Eph 4:3 (AMP) to "make every effort to keep the oneness of the Spirit in the bond of peace [each individual working together to make the whole successful]." Similarly, Jesus' high priestly prayer in John 17 expresses his longing that his followers would reflect the oneness he shares with the Father:

> I am praying not only for these disciples but also for all who will ever believe in me through their message. I pray that they will all be one, just as you and I are one—as you are in me, Father, and I am in you. And may they be in us so that the world will believe you sent me. (John 17:20–21)

Paul also exhorts the Philippians to cultivate this same spirit: ". . . agreeing wholeheartedly with each other, loving one another, and working together with one mind and purpose" (Phil 2:2).

God seems remarkably patient with the human imperfections that inevitably exist among his people. Despite the countless messes the church finds herself in, he covers her with grace and remains unwavering in his commitment to work through her to accomplish his purposes on the earth. Yet there appears to be at least one behavior that stirs a different response, where divine urgency replaces divine long-suffering: the breaking of oneness and the sowing of division. Such behavior is a violation of the love and oneness embodied within the Trinity and commanded among God's people. It undermines the very foundation upon which the church is meant to be built, reducing it to shifting sand. This may explain why Paul gives such strong instruction to Titus:

> If people are causing divisions among you, give a first and second warning. After that, have nothing more to do with them. For people like that have turned away from the truth, and their own sins condemn them. (Titus 3:10–11)

In 1 Cor 5:9–13, Paul adds sexual immorality to the list of behaviors serious enough to warrant separation between believers, while also clarifying that such boundaries are not meant for interactions with unbelievers. The takeaway is clear: oneness and purity within the church are not peripheral concerns—they are central to God's design for his people. The pioneering people of God—leaders and members alike—must remain vigilant against every offence and divisive spirit that threatens to undermine the work. Oneness must be actively cultivated, through the kinds of qualities outlined in Eph 4—such as commitment (verse 3), forgiveness (verses 2, 32), honest communication (verse 15), and meaningful contribution (verse 16).

Finally, *a pioneering spirit requires the courage to persevere through seasons of opposition and difficulty.* While the temple rebuilding begins with relative momentum in Ezra 3, chapter 4 quickly introduces significant resistance that threatens to derail the work. Throughout the chapter, the enemies of Judah and Benjamin employ strategies such as subtle manipulation, bribery, political petitioning of the Persian kings, and eventually, the use of force. Despite the perseverance of the Jewish remnant, the opposition eventually wore them down, and the final verse of chapter 4 records that the work came to a halt.

The words that follow offer an injection of hope amid the discouragement and beautifully illustrate the power of prophetic ministry: "At that time the prophets Haggai and Zechariah son of Iddo prophesied to the Jews in Judah and Jerusalem. They prophesied in the name of the God of Israel who was over them" (Ezra 5:1). It was to these battle-weary pioneers that Zechariah spoke his now-famous, soothing words: "It is not by force nor by strength, but by my Spirit, says the Lord of Heaven's Armies" (Zech 4:6), and, "Do not despise these small beginnings, for the Lord rejoices to see the work begin—to see the plumb line in Zerubbabel's hand" (Zech 4:10).

Haggai's prophecy in the opening chapter of his book offers one of the clearest contrasts between the human and divine perspectives during times of trial. He records God's assessment of the people's response: "This is what the Lord of Heaven's Armies says: The people are saying, 'The time has not yet come to rebuild the house of the Lord'" (Hag 1:2). In other words, the people interpreted the opposition as a sign they had misjudged the timing of God's assignment. But God saw it differently. In verses 3 to 6, Haggai reveals that the real issue was the people's shift in focus— from rebuilding the temple to building their own homes. God's instructions are direct: "This is what the Lord of Heaven's Armies says: Look at what's happening to you! Now go up into the hills, bring down timber, and rebuild my house. Then I will take pleasure in it and be honored, says the Lord" (Hag 1:7–8). To paraphrase: "I do not know why you stopped—I gave you clear instructions, and I am far more powerful than your enemies. Get back to work!"

Certainly, we all come to the end of ourselves in times of trial. But by the grace of God, he meets us in our weakness and speaks again—his word breathing fresh strength into weary hearts. That sacred wrestle, like Jacob contending with God at the ford of the Jabbok (Gen 32), must become an art form for pioneers—learning to push beyond the limits of human capacity and rise in the strength of divine resolve. This is what marked Zerubbabel, Jeshua, and the remnant who rose again to rebuild. And this must mark us too. In a post-COVID world, where the landscape is uncertain and the church's future contested, God is calling forth a resilient people—Spirit-led pioneers who will not shrink back but rise to build again.

Bibliography

Adams, Ken. "Two Questions Every Church Leader Ought to Be Asking." Impact Discipleship Ministries (blog), Oct. 28, 2020. https://impactdisciples.com/two-questions-every-church-leader-ought-to-be-asking/.

Adams, Tony E., et al. "Autoethnography." In *The International Encyclopedia of Communication Research Methods*, edited by Jörg Matthes et al., 1–11. Hoboken, NJ: Wiley, 2017.

Adamson, Dave. *Metachurch: How to Use Digital Ministry to Reach People and Make Disciples*. Cumming, GA: Orange, 2022.

Austin, Denise A., et al., eds. *Asia Pacific Pentecostalism*. Leiden: Brill, 2019.

Ball, Andrew J. "Christianity Incorporated: Sinclair Lewis and the Taylorization of American Protestantism." *Religion and Literature* 50 (2018) 65–90.

Barna Group. "One in Three Practicing Christians Has Stopped Attending Church During COVID-19." https://www.barna.com/research/new-sunday-morning-part-2/.

———. "Pastors Share Top Reasons They've Considered Quitting Ministry in the Past Year." https://www.barna.com/research/pastors-quitting-ministry/.

———. *Six Questions About the Future of the Hybrid Church Experience*. State of the Digital Church. Dallas, TX: Barna Group, 2020.

———. *The State of Discipleship*. Colorado Springs, CO: The Navigators, 2015.

Bartholomew, Craig. "Christ and Consumerism: An Introduction." In *Christ and Consumerism: Critical Reflections on the Spirit of Our Age*, edited by Craig Bartholomew and Thorsten Moritz, 1–12. Cumbria: Paternoster, 2000.

Bennett, Ron. *Intentional Disciplemaking: Cultivating Spiritual Maturity in the Local Church*. Colorado Springs, CO: NavPress, 2001. Kindle.

Berding, Kenneth. "What Does the Word 'Comfort' Mean in 2 Corinthians 1:3–7?" The Good Book Blog, Biola University, July 8, 2022. https://www.biola.edu/blogs/good-book-blog/2022/what-does-the-word-comfort-mean-in-2-corinthians-1-3-7.

Bernays, Edward L. *Propaganda*. New York: Liveright, 1928.

Beukes, Jacques W. "To Be or Not to Be? A Missional and Practical Theological Perspective on Being Church Without Walls Amidst Coronavirus Disease 2019: A Challenge or an Opportunity?" *HTS Teologiese Studies / Theological Studies* 76 (2020). https://doi.org/10.4102/hts.v76i1.6115.

Boca, Gratiela Dana. "Factors Influencing Students' Behavior and Attitude Towards Online Education During COVID-19." *Sustainability* 13.13 (2021) 1–21. https://doi.org/10.3390/su13137469.

Boni, Stefano. "The Era of Comfort, a Threat to Sufficiency?" *FACTS Reports* Special Issue 26 (2024) 50–53.

Borders, L. DiAnne, and Amanda L. Giordano. "Confronting Confrontation in Clinical Supervision: An Analytical Autoethnography." *Journal of Counseling and Development* 94 (2016) 454–63. https://doi.org/10.1002/jcad.12104.

Breen, Mike. *Building a Discipling Culture: How to Release a Missional Movement by Discipling People Like Jesus Did.* Pawley's Island, SC: 3DM International, 2017.

British Academy. "The COVID Decade: Understanding the Long-Term Societal Impacts of COVID-19." London: British Academy, 2021. https://doi.org/10.5871/bac19stf/9780856726583.001.

Brunsdon, Alfred R. "As We Were or Seeking What We Ought to Be? A Practical Theological Rethinking of the Communio Sanctorum in the Light of COVID-19." *Verbum et Ecclesia* 42 (2021) 1–9.

Burggraff, Andrew. "Developing Discipleship Curriculum: Applying the Systems Approach Model for Designing Instruction by Dick, Carey, and Carey to the Construction of Church Discipleship Courses." *Christian Education Journal* 12 (2015) 397–414.

Buys, P. J. "Reformation and Revival." *Haddington House Journal* 10 (2008) 163–92.

Caine, Christine. Foreword to *ReJesus*, by Michael Frost and Alan Hirsch, xiii–xv. Cody, WY: 100 Movements, 2022.

Carson, D. A. "Editorial: Why the Local Church Is More Important than TGC, White Horse Inn, 9Marks, and Maybe Even ETS." *Themelios* 40 (2015). https://www.thegospelcoalition.org/themelios/article/editorial-why-the-local-church-is-more-important-than-tgc-white-horse/.

Cettolin, Angelo Ulisse. *Spirit Freedom and Power: Changes in Pentecostal Spirituality.* Eugene, OR: Wipf and Stock, 2016. Kindle.

Chester, Tim. *A Meal with Jesus: Discovering Grace, Community, and Mission Around the Table.* Wheaton, IL: Crossway, 2011.

Clifton, Shane. *Pentecostal Churches in Transition: Analysing the Developing Ecclesiology of the Assemblies of God in Australia.* Leiden: Brill, 2009.

Comer, John Mark. *Practicing the Way: Be with Jesus. Become Like Him. Do As He Did.* La Vergne: SPCK, 2024.

Cordeiro, Wayne. *The Irresistible Church: 12 Traits of a Church Heaven Applauds.* Bloomington: Bethany House, 2011. Kindle.

Costea, Natanael. *19 Covid Lessons the Church Cannot Ignore: Why "Back to Normal" Is Not an Option.* San Giovanni Teatino: Evangelista, 2020.

Damazio, Frank. *Life Changing Leadership.* Grand Rapids: Baker, 2013.

Dames, Gordon. "'Quo Vadis' Practical Theology? A Response." *Scriptura* 100 (2009) 81–88.

Davis, J. Chase. *Trinitarian Formation: A Theology of Discipleship in Light of the Father, Son, and Holy Spirit.* Eugene, OR: Wipf and Stock, 2021.

Downie, Richard. "Kenya Under Growing Pressure to Regulate 'Spiritual Fraudsters.'" Sept. 23, 2019. https://www.csis.org/analysis/kenya-under-growing-pressure-regulate-spiritual-fraudsters.

Drucker, Peter. "Trusting the Teacher in the Grey-Flannel Suit." *Economist,* Nov. 17, 2005. https://www.economist.com/special-report/2005/11/17/trusting-the-teacher-in-the-grey-flannel-suit.

Dusting, Grant. "COVID Shows There Is Room for a New Reformation by a Re-Shaped Church." Nov. 17, 2020. https://www.eternitynews.com.au/australia/covid-shows-there-is-room-for-a-new-reformation-by-a-re-shaped-church/, https://www.eternitynews.com.au/australia/covid-shows-there-is-room-for-a-new-reformation-by-a-re-shaped-church/.

Dyer, John. "Exploring Mediated *Ekklesia*: How We Talk About Church in the Digital Age." In *Ecclesiology for a Digital Church: Theological Reflections on a New Normal,* edited by Heidi A. Campbell and John Dyer, 3–16. London: SCM, 2021.

Easley, Ray. "Theological Education and Leadership Development." *Renewal* 1.2 (2014) 4–26.

Eldredge, John. *Resilient: Restoring Your Weary Soul in These Turbulent Times.* Nashville: Nelson, 2022.

Ellis, Carolyn. *The Ethnographic I: A Methodological Novel About Autoethnography.* Ethnographic Alternatives 13. Walnut Creek, CA: AltaMira, 2004.

Ellis, Carolyn, et al. "Autoethnography: An Overview." *Historical Social Research / Historische Sozialforschung* 36.4 (2011) 273–90.

English, J. T. *Deep Discipleship: How the Church Can Make Whole Disciples of Jesus.* Nashville: B&H, 2020.

Eubanks, Olivia. "'Unprecedented' Named People's Choice 2020 Word of the Year by Dictionary.com." ABC News, Dec. 16, 2020. https://abcnews.go.com/Politics/unprecedented-named-peoples-choice-2020-word-year-dictionary/story?id=74735664.

Farahani, Mahboobe. "From Spoon Feeding to Self-Feeding: Are Iranian EFL Learners Ready to Take Charge of Their Own Learning?" *Electronic Journal of Foreign Language Teaching* 11 (2014) 98–115.

Farisani, Elelwani. "A Sociological Analysis of Israelites in Babylonian Exile." *Old Testament Essays* 17 (2004) 380–88.

Farrar Capon, Robert. *The Astonished Heart: Reclaiming the Good News from the Lost-and-Found of Church History.* Grand Rapids: Eerdmans, 1996.

Fensham, Frank Charles. *The Books of Ezra and Nehemiah.* The New International Commentary on the Old Testament. Grand Rapids: Eerdmans, 1982.

Fitch, David E. *The Great Giveaway*. Grand Rapids: Baker, 2005.

Flammang, Janet A. *Table Talk: Building Democracy One Meal at a Time*. Urbana, IL: University of Illinois Press, 2016.

Foster, Richard J. *Streams of Living Water*. New York: HarperCollins, 2010.

Friedman, Hershey, and Paul Hersovitz. "Rebuilding of the Temple and Renewal of Hope: Leadership Lessons from Zerubbabel, Ezra, and Nehemiah." *Journal of Values-Based Leadership* 12.2 (2019) 1–20. https://doi.org/10.22543/0733.122.1271.

Frost, Michael, and Alan Hirsch. *ReJesus: Remaking the Church in Our Founder's Image*. 2nd ed. Cody, WY: 100 Movements, 2022.

———. *The Shaping of Things to Come: Innovation and Mission for the 21st-Century Church*. Peabody, MA: Hendrickson, 2003.

Frost, Mike. "Coronavirus Could Set the Church Back 25 Years." Mike Frost (blog), Apr. 14, 2020. https://mikefrost.net/coronavirus-could-set-the-church-back-25-years/.

Gallaty, Robby. *Rediscovering Discipleship: Making Jesus' Final Words Our First Work*. Grand Rapids: Zondervan, 2015.

Geiger, Eric, et al. *Transformational Discipleship*. Nashville: B&H, 2012.

Gillette, J. Michael, and Rich Dionne. *Theatrical Design and Production: An Introduction to Scenic Design and Construction, Lighting, Sound, Costume, and Makeup*. 8th ed. New York: McGraw-Hill, 2020.

Gorrell, Angela Williams. "New Media and a New Reformation?" In *The Distanced Church: Reflections on Doing Church Online*, edited by Heidi A. Campbell, 58–60. College Station, TX: Digital Religions, 2020.

Grenz, Stanley J. *Theology for the Community of God*. Grand Rapids: Eerdmans, 2000.

Halter, Hugh, and Matt Smay. *AND: The Gathered and Scattered Church*. Grand Rapids: Zondervan, 2010.

Ham, Ken. "It's Time to Ignite a New Reformation!" Answers in Genesis, Oct. 30, 2017. https://answersingenesis.org/blogs/ken-ham/2017/10/30/its-time-ignite-new-reformation/.

Harrington, Bobby, and Alex Absalom. *Discipleship That Fits*. Grand Rapids: Zondervan, 2016.

Hartman, Laura M. *The Christian Consumer: Living Faithfully in a Fragile World*. New York: Oxford University Press, 2011.

Hayes, Andrew, and Stephen Cherry, eds. *The Meanings of Discipleship: Being Disciples Then and Now*. London: SCM, 2021.

Headspace. "Coping with COVID: The Mental Health Impact on Young People Accessing Headspace Services." Aug. 2020. https://headspace.org.au/assets/Uploads/COVID-Client-Impact-Report-FINAL-11-8-20.pdf.

Higgs, Kerryn. "A Brief History of Consumer Culture." The MIT Press Reader (blog), Jan. 11, 2021. https://thereader.mitpress.mit.edu/a-brief-history-of-consumer-culture/.

Hirsch, Alan. *The Forgotten Ways: Reactivating Apostolic Movements*. Grand Rapids: Brazos, 2016.

Hull, Bill. *Conversion and Discipleship: You Can't Have One Without the Other*. Grand Rapids: Zondervan, 2016.

———. *The Disciple-Making Church: Leading a Body of Believers on the Journey of Faith*. Updated ed. Grand Rapids: Baker, 2010.

Jennings, Marianna M. "In Defense of the Sage on the Stage: Escaping from the 'Sorcery' of Learning Styles and Helping Students Learn How to Learn." *Journal of Legal Studies Education* 29 (2012) 191–237.

Jiang, Xin. "Strategic Management for Main Functional Areas in an Organization." *International Journal of Business and Management* 4 (2009) 153–57.

John, Neetu, et al. "Lessons Never Learned: Crisis and Gender-Based Violence." *Developing World Bioethics* 20.2 (2020) 65–68. https://doi.org/10.1111/dewb.12261.

Johnston, Erin F., et al. "Pastoral Ministry in Unsettled Times: A Qualitative Study of the Experiences of Clergy During the COVID-19 Pandemic." *Review of Religious Research* 64 (2022) 375–97. https://doi.org/10.1007/s13644-021-00465-y.

Kaunda, Chammah J. "The Need to Rethink African 'Ideas of Christ' in the Search for Human Flouring in Post-Covid-19 Era." *Dialog* 60 (2021) 322–30. https://doi.org/10.1111/dial.12661.

Kitchen, K. A. *On the Reliability of the Old Testament*. Grand Rapids: Eerdmans, 2003.

Kramer, Michael W. "Sage on the Stage or Bore at the Board?" *Communication Education* 66 (2017) 245–47.

Kreglinger, Gisela H. *The Spirituality of Wine*. Grand Rapids: Eerdmans, 2016.

Krispin, Keith R. "Christian Leader Development: An Outcomes Framework." *Christian Education Journal: Research on Educational Ministry* 17 (2020) 18–37. https://doi.org/10.1177/0739891319869697.

Le Duc, Anthony. "The Church's Online Presence and Ecclesial Communion: Virtual or Real?" In *Ecclesiology for a Digital Church: Theological Reflections on a New Normal*, edited by Heidi A. Campbell and John Dyer, 17–32. London: SCM, 2021.

Lee, Kyuboem. "How Might the COVID-19 Crisis Reshape Our Churches for Good?" *Christianity Today*, 2021. https://www.christianitytoday.com/pastors/2021/fall/how-might-covid-19-crisis-reshape-our-churches-for-good.html.

Lefebvre, Solange. "What the COVID-19 Pandemic Has Revealed About Religions." *Religions* 13.6 (2022) 1–5. https://doi.org/10.3390/rel13060550.

Liang, Yaodong, et al. "Mental Health Research During the COVID-19 Pandemic: Focuses and Trends." *Frontiers in Public Health* 10 (2022) 1–12. https://doi.org/10.3389/fpubh.2022.895121.

Li, Wei. "Racial Disparities in COVID-19." Harvard University (website), Oct. 24, 2020. https://sitn.hms.harvard.edu/flash/2020/racial-disparities-in-covid-19/.

Malphurs, Aubrey. *Advanced Strategic Planning: A 21st-Century Model for Church and Ministry Leaders.* 3rd ed. Grand Rapids: Baker, 2013.

———. *Strategic Disciple Making: A Practical Tool for Successful Ministry.* Grand Rapids: Baker, 2009.

Malphurs, Aubrey, and Steve Stoope. *Money Matters in Church: A Practical Guide for Leaders.* Grand Rapids: Baker, 2011.

Marshall, Katherine. "COVID-19 and Religion: Pandemic Lessons and Legacies." *Review of Faith and International Affairs* 20.4 (2022) 80–90. https://doi.org/10.1080/15570274.2022.2139523.

Mathews, Shailer. *Scientific Management in the Churches.* Chicago: University of Chicago Press, 1912.

McCracken, Brett. "The Digital Revolution Reformation." Gospel Coalition, Nov. 19, 2019. https://www.thegospelcoalition.org/article/digital-revolution-reformation/.

———. "8 Signs Your Christianity Is Too Comfortable." Gospel Coalition, Oct. 24, 2017. https://www.thegospelcoalition.org/article/8-signs-your-christianity-is-too-comfortable/.

———. *Uncomfortable: The Awkward and Essential Challenge of Christian Community.* Wheaton, IL: Crossway, 2017.

McGrath, Alister E. *Reformation Thought: An Introduction.* 4th ed. Malden, MA: Wiley-Blackwell, 2012. Scribd.

McKnight, Scot, and Laura McKnight Barringer. *A Church Called Tov: Forming a Goodness Culture That Resists Abuses of Power and Promotes Healing.* Carol Stream, IL: Tyndale House, 2020.

Miller, Jason A., and Judy L. Glanz. "The Personal Experiences of Pastoral Leaders During the COVID-19 Quarantine." *Christian Education Journal: Research on Educational Ministry* 18 (2021) 500–518. https://doi.org/10.1177/07398913211048909.

Mooallem, Jon. "Three Years into Covid, We Still Don't Know How to Talk About It." Photographs by Ashley Gilbertson. *New York Times,* Feb. 22, 2023. https://www.nytimes.com/interactive/2023/02/22/magazine/covid-pandemic-oral-history.html.

Mpofu, Buhle. "Mission on the Margins: A Proposal for an Alternative Missional Paradigm in the Wake of COVID-19." *HTS Teologiese Studies / Theological Studies* 76 (2020) 1–6. https://doi.org/10.4102/hts.v76i1.6149.

Murrell, Steve. *WikiChurch.* Lake Mary, FL: Charisma House, 2011.

Norsworthy, Beverley, et al. "Learning and Loves Envisaged Through the Lens of James K. A. Smith: Reimagining Christian Education Today." In *Reimagining Christian Education: Cultivating Transformative Approaches,* edited by Johannes M. Luetz et al., 3–16. Singapore: Springer Nature, 2018.

Ogden, Greg. *The New Reformation.* Grand Rapids: Zondervan, 1990.

———. *Transforming Discipleship: Making Disciples a Few at a Time.* Downers Grove, IL: IVP, 2016.

Osmer, Richard Robert. *Practical Theology: An Introduction.* Grand Rapids: Eerdmans, 2008.

Oxford Languages. *2020: Words of an Unprecedented Year*. 2020. https://languages.oup.com/wp-content/uploads/oxford-languages-words-of-an-unprecedented-year-2020.pdf.

Patrick, Darrin. "Control Tweaks." *Christianity Today*. https://www.christianitytoday.com/pastors/2010/spring/controltweaks.html.

Peterson, Eugene H. *The Pastor: A Memoir*. New York: HarperCollins, 2011.

Pillay, Jerry. "COVID-19 Shows the Need to Make Church More Flexible." *Transformation: An International Journal of Holistic Mission Studies* 37.4 (2020) 266–75.

Putman, Jim. *Real-Life Discipleship: Building Churches That Make Disciples*. Colorado Springs, CO: NavPress, 2010.

Putman, Jim, and Bobby Harrington. *DiscipleShift*. Grand Rapids: Zondervan, 2013.

Rainer, Thom S. *The Post-Quarantine Church: Six Urgent Challenges and Opportunities That Will Determine the Future of Your Congregation*. Carol Stream, IL: Tyndale House, 2020.

———. *Simple Church in a Post-COVID World*. N.p., X.Church, 2021.

Reeves, Michael. *The Good God*. Milton Keynes: Paternoster, 2012. Kindle.

Roy, Arundhati. "The Pandemic Is a Portal." *Financial Times*, Apr. 3, 2020. https://www.ft.com/content/10d8f5e8-74eb-11ea-95fe-fcd274e920ca.

Russ, Eric. *Discipleship Defined*. Maitland, FL: Xulon, 2010. Kindle.

Ryken, Philip Graham. *City on a Hill: Reclaiming the Biblical Pattern for the Church in the 21st Century*. Chicago: Moody, 2003.

Sanders, Fred. "Follow the Trinity by Following Christ." Gospel Coalition, May 28, 2021. https://www.thegospelcoalition.org/article/discipleship-trinitarian-key/.

Sargeant, Kimon H. *Seeker Churches: Promoting Traditional Religion in a Nontraditional Way*. Sociology of Religion. New Brunswick, NJ: Rutgers University Press, 2000. Kindle.

Schaller, Lyle E. *New Reformation*. Nashville: Abingdon, 1987.

Spader, Dann. *4 Chair Discipling: What He Calls Us to Do*. Chicago: Moody, 2019.

Sparks, Larry (@lsparks3). "'How was worship?' Must be removed from our Christian vernacular. 'How was worship?' Is a question only the object of our worship can answer." Instagram photo, June 17, 2021. https://www.instagram.com/p/CQOTx48sNtH/?hl=en.

Stafford, Tim. "Died: Robert Schuller, Forerunner of the Seeker-Sensitive Movement." *Christianity Today*, Apr. 2, 2015. https://www.christianitytoday.com/ct/2015/april-web-only/died-robert-schuller-forerunner-of-seeker-sensitive-movemen.html.

Stahl, Florian, et al. "The Impact of Brand Equity on Customer Acquisition, Retention, and Profit Margin." *Journal of Marketing* 76.4 (2012) 44–63.

Stiles, J. Mack. *Evangelism: How the Whole Church Speaks of Jesus*. Wheaton, IL: Crossway, 2014.

Stott, John R. W. *The Message of Ephesians*. London: IVP, 2020.

Suidan Al Badi, Khalid. "The Impact of Marketing Mix on the Competitive Advantage of the SME Sector in the Al Buraimi Governorate in Oman." *SAGE Open* 8.3 (2018) 1–10.

Svob, Connie, et al. "Pre- and Post-Pandemic Religiosity and Mental Health Outcomes: A Prospective Study." *International Journal of Environmental Research and Public Health* 20.11 (2023) 1–14. https://doi.org/10.3390/ijerph20116002.

Sweet, Leonard. "From Semiotic Exegesis to Contextual Ecclesiology: The Hermeneutics of Missional Faith in the COVIDian Era." *HTS Teologiese Studies / Theological Studies* 77.4 (2021) 1–14.

———. *From Tablet to Table.* Colorado Springs, CO: NavPress, 2014.

Swinton, John, and Harriet Mowatt. *Practical Theology and Qualitative Research.* 2nd ed. London: SCM, 2016.

Tidball, Derek. *Skilful Shepherds: Explorations in Pastoral Theology.* Leicester: Apollos, 1997.

Valdes, Kristin. "Reflection and Change in Unprecedented Times." *Journal of Hand Therapy* 35 (2022) 160–63.

Vaters, Karl. "Pastoring After COVID." Influence, Jan. 13, 2021. https://influencemagazine.com/en/practice/pastoring-after-covid.

———. "The Unexpected Origins of the Church Growth Movement, with Dr. Gary McIntosh." Episode 27 in *Can This Work in a Small Church?* Karl Vaters (website), June 6, 2022. https://karlvaters.com/gary-mcintosh-podcast-ep-027/.

Verster, Pieter. "Rebuilding the Community and the Church Post-COVID-19." *Pharos Journal of Theology* 102 (2021) 1–12.

Wells, David F. *God in the Wasteland: The Reality of Truth in a World of Fading Dreams.* Grand Rapids: Eerdmans, 1994. Kindle.

White, Ellen G. *Selected Messages Book 1.* Silver Spring, MD: Ellen G. White Estate, 2010.

Wilk, Richard. "Consumption, Human Needs, and Global Environmental Change." *Global Environmental Change* 12 (2002) 5–13. https://doi.org/10.1016/S0959-3780(01)00028-0.

Wilkins, Michael J. *Following the Master: Biblical Theology of Discipleship.* Grand Rapids: Zondervan, 1992.

Willard, Dallas. *The Great Omission: Reclaiming Jesus's Essential Teachings on Discipleship.* Oxford: Monarch, 2006.

Willett, Don. "A Biblical Model of Stages of Spiritual Development: The Journey According to John." *Journal of Spiritual Formation and Soul Care* 3 (2010) 88–102.

Wilson, Jared C. *The Gospel-Driven Church: Uniting Church Growth Dreams with the Metrics of Grace.* Unabridged ed. Grand Rapids: Zondervan, 2019.

———. *The Prodigal Church: A Gentle Manifesto Against the Status Quo.* Wheaton, IL: Crossway, 2015.

Wise, Jacqui. "Covid-19: WHO Declares End of Global Health Emergency." *BMJ* 381 (2023) 1041. https://doi.org/10.1136/bmj.p1041.

World Justice Project. *The COVID-19 Pandemic and the Global Justice Gap.* Oct. 2020. https://worldjusticeproject.org/sites/default/files/documents/Global%20Justice%20Gap-11-02.pdf.

World Relief. "The COVID-19 Impact on World's Poor." Mar. 2022. https://worldrelief.org/content/uploads/2022/03/WR-COVIDReport_Executive-Summary.pdf.

Yan, Zheng. "Unprecedented Pandemic, Unprecedented Shift, and Unprecedented Opportunity." *Human Behavior and Emerging Technologies* 2 (2020) 110–12. https://doi.org/10.1002/hbe2.192.

Zandroto, Iman Jaya. "COVID-19 and the Mission of the Church: Some Notes on the New Normal." *International Bulletin of Mission Research* 45 (2021) 346–54. https://doi.org/10.1177/23969393211034603.

Zhao, Yixuan, et al. "COVID-19 and Mental Health in Australia—A Scoping Review." *BMC Public Health* 22.1200 (2022) 1–13. https://doi.org/10.1186/s12889-022-13527-9.

www.ingramcontent.com/pod-product-compliance
Lightning Source LLC
Chambersburg PA
CBHW071100090426
42737CB00013B/2397